"I must... ...for the fog is r... *Emily Dickinson*

"When you come to the hedge — that we all must go over — it isn't so bad. **You feel sleepy — and you don't care.** Just a little dreamy anxiety — which world you're really in — that's all." —Stephen Crane

"I want to sleep now." —Lord Byron

"Carry my bones before you on your march, for the rebels will not be able to endure the sight of me, alive or dead."

—*Edward I*

Goodbye, all that is charming, goodly, wit and gaiety, goodbye, you merry friends, for I am dying and wishing to see you soon contented in another life!" —Miguel de Cervantes

"I don't know what I may seem to the world. But as to myself, I seem to have been only a boy playing in the seashore and diverting myself . . . whilst the great ocean of truth lay all undiscovered before me."

—*Sir Isaac Newton*

want to sleep now." —Lord Byron

ENCYCLOPEDIA of The End

DEBORAH NOYES

ENCYCLOPEDIA

of

The End

MYSTERIOUS DEATH

in

FACT, FANCY, FOLKLORE,

and MORE

HOUGHTON MIFFLIN COMPANY

BOSTON 2008

www.houghtonmifflinbooks.com

The text of this book is set in Guardi Roman.
Book design by Michael Nelson

Library of Congress Cataloging-in-Publication Data
Noyes, Deborah.
Encyclopedia of the end : mysterious death in fact, fancy,
folklore, and more / by Deborah Noyes.
p. cm.
ISBN 978-0-618-82362-8
1. Death—Social aspects. 2. Funeral rites and ceremonies. I. Title.
HQ1073.N68 2008
306.903-dc22
2008001872

Manufactured in China
SCP 10 9 8 7 6 5 4 3 2 1

For Elizabeth Washak,
a.k.a. "the Heat"
1932–1993

"TO DIE WILL BE AN AWFULLY
BIG ADVENTURE."

~Peter Pan

INTRODUCTION

ONCE YOU'VE SIGNED ON TO WRITE A BOOK ABOUT DEATH, there comes a day when you say, "Enough death already," and vow to leave the whole bleak business behind. This suits your friends and family, who've done a lot of coughing into their fists lately during conversation. It also makes you feel like a quitter. So you dust off the research books and brave the keyboard again. Death is *interesting*, you remind yourself. Death is *important*.

One such reluctant day, a damp day in early spring, I arrived to photograph an old New England graveyard, expecting the familiar scene of serene abandonment. Instead I found a field trip—some three dozen raucous kids—racing between the graves in bright raincoats. They made charcoal rubbings and stroked angel heads or skulls carved into the mossy, tilting stones while their chaperones gossiped with crossed arms.

Derailed by shrieks and laughter, I kneeled by a sunken grave and read the epitaph for a child who'd died in 1813, at age fifteen months:

> Lie still sweet babe & take thy rest
> God call'd you home He thought it best.

I watched as the earth around the stone rose slightly under wet leaves and dandelion greens—some busy animal moving below the surface, a mole or vole or gopher. Sparrows rose and darted from stone to stone. Great old beech trees stood like patient watchers, damp boughs spread in welcome. Ha! I thought. Life. Right here in Death's neighborhood. Right under Death's nose.

But like the burrowing animal and the birds and the busy children, the dead, hunkered under centuries of history, seemed no less a part of everything. Here they were, after all, hosting a fine day out for rambunctious third graders.

There's an old saying, "Death and the sun are not to be looked at steadily." In the twenty-first century, this holds truer than ever. Many Americans have never laid eyes on a dead body. If they have seen one, it was in a mortician's parlor—painted and powdered and poked through with fluids, far removed from the familiar and dear, from the person now departed.

Death is a mystery so vast, so full of puzzle and paradox that we turn our eyes from it. That said, questions bubble below the surface of our thoughts. Do bodies house souls? If so, where does the body end and the soul begin? *Is* death an end? Or a beginning? Why are we as eager to appease as memorialize our dead, and why fear as much as grieve them?

A book like this can't be exhaustive, but here you'll find facts and fancy, rites and anecdotes on topics from the afterlife to atheism, mediums to morticians, hungry ghosts to grave robbers. I hope they're related with awe and respect but also with a hint of irreverence. I hope, too, that the encyclopedic format encourages readers to browse and, if need be, take on just a little of an all-too-large subject at a time, and perhaps explore all the many related topics I haven't yet discovered or couldn't include.

We all die. This knowledge, say the spiritually wise, is the key to life. The great sculptor Michelangelo once proclaimed, "No thought exists in me which death has not carved with his chisel."

Life matters because it's on loan. If we had all the time in the world, would we care how we spent it? Since time *is* of the essence, it can't hurt to welcome death into our thoughts now and then as cultures of the past have done, as the surest way of honoring life.

The old memento mori tradition once urged: *Remember to die.* Of course, these words really mean, Be mindful. Remember to live.

AMULET

Amulets are good luck charms or protective talismans carried or worn by the living as jewelry. In ancient Egypt, they were also affixed to the dead. Embalmers layered amulets under bandages as they wrapped the body, reciting spells to shield the mummy and help trigger rebirth in the afterworld. Many amulets were crafted in the image of gods or in tribute to the gods' magical abilities. The scarab or dung beetle stood for Khepri, god of resurrection, because it lays its eggs in animal waste, an apt metaphor for life rising out of death. The *udjat* eye was a powerful magical shield aligning the wearer with the god Horus, who lost his eye in battle and later had it restored.

Egyptian amulets were crafted of everything from porcelain and glass to gold, silver, and semiprecious stones, so were at least as likely to imperil as to protect a mummy. Tomb robbers regularly ripped up mummies in search of valuable amulets and other treasure. See also: *Embalming, Mummy.*

ANCESTOR WORSHIP
(OR *VENERATION*)

Ancestor worship is one of the most common forms of human religious expression. Whether once alive and now joined with the community of the dead, or spirit beings that never inhabited this plane at all, ancestors are a society's most revered members, eclipsing even living elders in wisdom and power.

The dead are thought of as individuals at first but are eventually absorbed into and prayed to as a group. In East Asia each family might keep soul tablets of the recently dead lined up on a family altar, but that same altar is a way to contact all the ancestors and inform them of birthdays, weddings, and other key family events.

Ancestors keep a keen watch on their descendants, offering advice and protection to the

Ancestral tablet of wood covered with black, gold, and red paint, China.

living, bearing gifts and magical aid, so they demand care and respect in return. To deprive them of offerings is to risk their displeasure or wrath. They are keepers of lore, witnesses to the past, guardians of the future. They can both bless and curse.

In Africa, woodcarvers made ancestor figures as a place where the spirits of the dead could live. In many African cultures, distant ancestors form the most senior level of a society constructed of spirits, sorcerers, ghosts, and humans. They might watch over an entire clan or tribe, as powerful as gods, given to anger when disrespected.

For many ethnic groups in Madagascar, ancestors control human destiny. Festive death ceremonies—including burial, disinterment, and reburial—are serious social and cultural events on the island. Relatives might even spirit the remains of an ancestor away to a village dance or a soccer game before returning the bones to the family tomb.

See also: *Appeasing the dead, Burial—second, Hereafter.*

ANGEL OF DEATH

In ancient Hebrew literature, God, called Yahweh, dispensed death but didn't necessarily interact with humans. So the "Angel of Yahweh" acted as His agent. In later Jewish folklore the dark angel is named Sammael, meaning the "drug of God," since his sword was tipped with poison. Howling dogs marked his coming.

In Islamic tradition, the angel of death is not the same as Death, who's personified separately. In the Book of Resurrection, ultimate responsibility lies with God, but an angel named Izrail (or Azrael) stands watch under a tree in the shadow of God's throne. Forty days before a person is fated to die, a leaf with his name on it falls from the tree. A recording angel informs Izrail, who descends with the figure of Death to the chosen, and the two reveal themselves. Izrail is the last sight each mortal sees and in some accounts he's as tall as the span between earth and heaven. Medieval paintings show him with a foot resting on the bridge that links heaven and hell, over which those who are to be judged must pass. His wingspan is tremendous, embracing the virtuous and obliterating the wicked. In yet other accounts he has four faces, thousands of wings, and a body covered in tongues and eyes. Izrail may be accompanied by two sets of angels: those on his right, who tend the souls of the chosen, glow with radiance, and smell sweet; those on his left have black faces, glowing red eyes, and booming voices, and emit a noxious odor as they lead the wicked to a fiery fate.

See also: *Death—personified.*

APPEASING THE DEAD

In the folklore of many cultures, the time between death and burial is downright dangerous and the deceased a source of dread. Today we perform death rites out of grief, affection, and respect for those we've lost. But according to anthropologists, many traditions have their origins in fear, and we're motivated by self-preservation as much as sentiment.

No matter how dearly beloved, a person's "loosening" spirit may prove jealous, spiteful, resistant, angry—and wrong ritual, or none at all, can leave that spirit stranded between the here and the hereafter. Instead of passing uneventfully on, the spirit stays and plagues the living. Ghastly hangers-on —*doppelgängers,* hungry ghosts, banshees, poltergeists, vampires, zombies— occur in nearly every tradition, with the undead sharing certain universal traits. Most often, they died violently, abruptly, or with significant unfinished business, so these "high risk" corpses were treated with special care. In ancient and medieval Europe and elsewhere, plague and murder victims, suicides, mothers claimed in childbirth, lovers taken on the brink of marriage, and other dangerous dead might be confined to water, a ditch, bog, or remote cave, or buried at borderlines and crossroads to confound them and prevent them from finding their way back.

It's widely held that the dead must be properly handled. A corpse should be removed from the place of death and later from the home carefully. When lost souls venture back, they must travel exactly the way they came, so raising the threshold and carrying the corpse under instead of over it or removing the body through a window or a hole cut in the wall prohibits reentry.

A dead body must be covered until safely buried or disposed of. Rotting or "changing" flesh *looks* animated, and some traditions believed the mere appearance of life might reanimate the body.

The dead also have physical danger spots, as wandering spirits might return or invade through the mouth, eyes, nostrils, and other orifices. Egyptians stuffed the mouths of mummies with wool. Because meeting the gaze of the dead could be deadly, many cultures sealed closed the eyes, stopping them up with wax, pinning them shut with needles. Feet were tied together to prevent the Devil or evil spirits from entering the body. Feet and hands were also trouble, as they made for mobility. In Greek folklore, murder victims and executed criminals—those most likely to return—had these extremities cut off and strung round their necks on chains as a preventive measure.

Death rituals in Ireland, northern England, Australia, and elsewhere caution against leaving the body alone. A sympathetic someone should watch over it day and night. A wake ensures that the dead really *are* dead but also, ironically, persuades them they're still alive. Mirrors are turned toward the wall, clocks stopped, windows opened to allow the ghost to go. Friends and loved ones may touch the body a final time to ward off dreams of the dead.

Historically, people have appeased, soothed, confused, and guided the newly dead in many ways. To prove that death has taken place, salute the departing spirit, or frighten off evil spirits that might attempt to inhabit the body, mourners might make a racket to alert the dead that it's time to "go": in ancient Rome they loosed a *conclamatio mortis,* or death shout. Other traditions tolled bells, beat gongs, fired guns, or wailed and praised to demonstrate suitable regret. Another method was to dance, sing, or otherwise stage a show of merriment to trick and distract the departed from all they'd lost. Measures like these were taken until the dead could be safely buried and ritually "released."

Water, light, flame, smoke, and incense cajole, corral, or distract a detached spirit and tempt it away from the corpse and bereft loved ones. Water poured behind the coffin creates a magical barrier, for the dead are drawn to water and won't cross over, while light or flame draws the soul out and prevents anything else from slipping *in,* hence the candles in funeral processions (for Christians, the sign of the cross serves the same purpose).

Often the dead are buried with objects or items to support, placate, or occupy them. These grave goods might include transportation in the form of a boat, food and drink, even sacrificed loved ones, servants, or pets. In northern Germany the dead were evidently obsessed with untying knots, so people buried them with nets to keep them occupied.

Dark mourning clothes conceal the living. Flowers mollify. Wreaths encircle and entrap. Stones—from the heaviest tombstone to the tiny pebbles that mourners lay on graves when they visit cemeteries—hold the dead below the earth.
See also: *Food—for the dead, Funerary rites, Grave goods, Light, Mirrors, Mourning dress, Superstition, Undead, Wake, Water.*

ARS MORIENDI

Ars Moriendi, books on the art of dying, were popular in Europe and Britain in the fifteenth and sixteenth centuries. Dying a "good death," claimed these how-to books with a holy purpose, was as much an art as living a virtuous life. According to tomes like *The Book of the Craft of Dying and Other English Tracts Concerning Death* and *The Rules and Exercises of Holy Dying,* the Devil made a real lunge for your soul at the end, and you needed

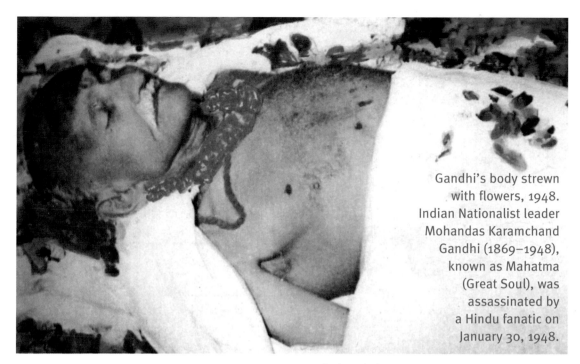

Gandhi's body strewn with flowers, 1948. Indian Nationalist leader Mohandas Karamchand Gandhi (1869–1948), known as Mahatma (Great Soul), was assassinated by a Hindu fanatic on January 30, 1948.

faith, strength, purity, and all the help you could get to weather temptation and terror, and to slip past with your soul intact. To get your earthly and spiritual affairs in order you followed a series of steps: preparing a will, confessing and repenting of sins, receiving absolution from a priest or minister, and so on.

To drive home the perils of avoidance, the woodcuts in these handy guidebooks illustrated the dangers of a "bad" death with the wicked writhing in torment while their souls—too late—intuit their fate. One book depicts the trials of an Everyman named Moriens on his deathbed, surrounded by swarms of demons jockeying to snatch his soul. The *Ars Moriendi* tradition died out in the Renaissance, as science and the Industrial Revolution encouraged more "enlightened" or rational views and improved the conditions of everyday life. See also: *Dance of death, Memento mori.*

ASSASSINATION

From Jesus Christ and Roman emperor Julius Caesar to activist Martin Luther King, Jr., and Prime Minister Yitzhak Rabin of Israel, assassination—the murder of a public figure to effectively change the course of history—has served as a violent tool of political power. Some assassins kill in service of a group or ideology; others just want power, period. Some are madmen seeking notoriety; others, known as hit men or contract killers, kill on demand for money.

In some cases the motive is straightforward. Charlotte Corday killed radical French revolutionary Jean-Paul Marat in 1793 supposedly as a patriotic act. Other assassinations, like that of U.S. president John F. Kennedy, are harder to explain and spawn copious theories. Whatever the goal, an assassination may have next to no significant impact, may backfire by making a martyr of the fallen, or may set off a chain of major events. In Europe, the murder of Archduke Franz Ferdinand by Serb insurgents, coming on the heels of years of escalating conflict, triggered World War I.

In the Middle Ages many European nobles, fearing the machinations of rivals, avoided the problem of poisoning by ordering their meals placed on a special table. Before food entered the VIP digestive tract, it was tasted by an unlucky servant. If the taster survived, the meal could be served with confidence, which is how the Italian version of that word, *credenza,* got to be a synonym for side table.

Another line of defense is to staff bodyguards, though disloyalty from within can be the greatest danger of all. Indian prime minister Indira Gandhi was assassinated in 1984 by two of her Sikh bodyguards.

In modern times, as global political divisions and stakes grew in scale, assassinations picked up. In Russia alone, four emperors were murdered in a span of not quite two hundred years, and U.S. presidents Abraham Lincoln, James Garfield, William McKinley, and John F. Kennedy all died at the hands of assassins.
See also: *Murder.*

ATHEISM (AND DEATH)
The absence of belief in God—or the active belief that no God or gods exist—was rare in Europe throughout the Middle Ages, when religion and all things metaphysical held center stage. But by

the Renaissance, people like Leonardo da Vinci were experimenting with skeptical inquiry and fielding arguments from religious authorities. It was only during the seventeenth and eighteenth centuries, Karen Armstrong says in her book *A History of God,* that "people in the West would cultivate an attitude that would make the denial of God's existence not only possible but desirable. They would find support for their views in science."

Throughout the Enlightenment, many prominent thinkers considered the natural world to be the basis of everything and denied the existence of God or immortality. Late in the nineteenth century, atheism got a boost from rational, freethinking philosophers like Friedrich Nietzsche, who famously declared God "dead," while in the twentieth century, the Soviet Union and other Communist states enshrined atheism and opposed religion, at times with violence. State atheism prevailed in the USSR until the Soviet Union dissolved.

Modern scientists like Albert Einstein and Stephen Hawking have often referred to God in a metaphorical or poetic way. In a BBC interview broadcast in 2004, Oxford professor Richard Dawkins, who later authored a bestselling book called *The God Delusion,* said, "Einstein's God, which simply means the laws of nature which are so deeply mysterious that they inspire a feeling of reverence—I believe in that, but I wouldn't call it God."

A central premise of atheism is the

idea that death is the end of human existence, and it's often joked that "there are no atheists in a foxhole." But for the majority of nonbelievers, who don't hedge their bets at death's door, what does the end look like?

A nonreligious or humanist funeral, conducted by a secular officiant—someone familiar with the procedures of cremation and burial who can be sensitive without invoking religion—might look a bit like a church service with music, readings of poetry and prose that reflect on death or celebrate and honor the life of the departed, a eulogy focusing on his or her achievements, and formal words of goodbye. Candle lighting and moments of silence and reflection, during which religious survivors can pray, are also common.

The writer and naturalist Edward Abbey, who died in 1989, is reputedly buried in an unmarked desert grave somewhere in southern Arizona. Before the fact he asked that his body be transported in the bed of a pickup truck. He wanted no undertakers, no embalming, no coffin—just an old sleeping bag. Ignore state laws concerning burial, he urged, and for a graveside ceremony stage a night of gunfire and bagpipes, with beer and booze and chili, and lots of singing, dancing, laughing, and hollering. Much of which transpired, so the story goes, with a friend blowing taps on a trumpet all the while.

And after that?

Abbey claimed in his book *Desert Solitaire* that he wasn't so much an atheist as "an earthiest," sworn to the natural world. His wish for his own death? "If my decomposing carcass helps nourish the roots of a juniper tree or the wings of a vulture—that is immortality enough for me. And as much as anyone deserves."

AUTOPSY
(OR *POSTMORTEM*)

An autopsy is a medical examination of a corpse done by a forensic pathologist. Usually autopsies are performed to find or confirm cause of death, establish identity, or determine proper medical care. They're also carried out for scientific study.

While pathologists work they jot down notes, scribble diagrams, and take photos or x-rays, especially if the death in question is linked to a crime.

An autopsy begins with a Y-shaped incision, one cut each from shoulder or armpit. The cuts meet beneath the breastbone, with the incision proceeding down to the middle of the abdomen above the genitals. The pathologist removes the front of the ribs and breastbone, extracts and examines internal organs, and then slices behind the ears and across the scalp, easing the front of the scalp over the face and the back down to the nape of the neck. Using a high-speed saw, she makes a cut in the skull to look inside for signs of swelling, injury, or infection. Lastly she sends tissue and fluid samples on to a lab for analysis.

The word "autopsy" means "seeing for oneself," and the roots of the procedure can be traced back more than five thousand years to the ancient Babylonians, who believed they could read the future in the entrails—especially the liver, considered the home of the soul—of animal sacrifices. Their observations were religious, not scientific, in nature, but like those of the ancient Egyptians (who mastered the techniques of embalming), they contributed to our later grasp of anatomy and showed how autopsy might help trace the cause and nature of disease.

The ancient Greeks, who thought disease was caused by disturbed proportions of fluids in the body, neglected solid anatomy. They saw the body and soul as separate entities, so dissection was acceptable, but already in the fourth century BC, there was controversy brewing. Hippocrates, the father of medicine and no fan of the practice, called autopsy "an unpleasant, if not cruel, task." The famous Greek anatomist Galen, whose work in the second century influenced the study of anatomy for nearly 1,400 years, depended almost entirely on pigs and monkeys for his research.

One celebrated early autopsy took place in 44 BC in ancient Rome. After dictator Julius Caesar was stabbed to death in the Senate house by a number of his friends and senators, a physician named Antistius determined that only one of the twenty-three stab wounds actually caused his death.

But for centuries after Caesar's murder, autopsies were unpopular or illegal because of widespread belief in keeping the dead intact, and scientists were limited to dissecting animals.

In the late fifteenth century, Leonardo da Vinci furtively made use of human cadavers for his anatomical drawings, depicting the human skeletal, muscular, and vascular systems as never before. Taboos were loosening, thanks to the vigorous influence of science during the Renaissance, but with corpses hard to come by (who wanted their body violated after death?), body snatching became a cottage industry.

Eventually, as legal consent became necessary for dissection, the public began to tolerate the practice. Attitudes toward death shifted yet again during World War I. With so many soldiers lost in the trenches, society learned to separate the whereabouts of a body from a soul's fate in the afterlife, and medical schools began to receive a steady supply of donated corpses.

Despite taboos, people have been peering inside bodies for thousands of years, and their drawings and written observations have helped doctors through the ages learn about human anatomy.

Paleopathologists examine ancient corpses, skeletons, and mummies.
See also: *Body snatching, Causes of death, Corpse, Forensic science.*

BARROW

A tomb where the earth is heaped up over a dead body. A barrow may be large or small, anything from the vast mounds over great megalithic tombs to a modest pile of dirt raised over an individual grave.

Many barrows had tunnel entrances where the dead—sometimes many (the entrance tunnel would be sealed with earth after each fresh burial and dug out again as needed)—were placed with their belongings. In Germanic, Scandinavian, Irish, Gallic, and Anglo-Saxon traditions, the barrow wasn't just a burial site; it was a place for the dead to dwell. They were perceived as sitting inside, keeping fierce watch over their wealth and weapons.

The old Anglo-Saxon hero Beowulf asked to be buried in a mound on a steep headland so passing sailors could witness his fame, and many barrows were positioned on lonely cliffs overlooking the sea.

See also: *Grave, Hereafter, Tomb.*

✦ ✦ ✦

BEES AND HIVES

Bees and people have a long history together, and in British folklore, that bond continues on even in death. Until sugar was imported to rural England and elsewhere, honey was the sole sweetening agent humans had. It was also used to help ferment cider, ale, and mead, so honey and bees were precious. Country folk in England called bees "the little servants of God" and believed they could see the future, making it unlucky to kill them.

Many churches kept beehives to supply wax for the dark yellow candles used in funeral masses. Annual ceremonial prayers might be said for bees to thank them for their industry and for the promise of light throughout the coming year. Many parishioners willed money (or even beehives) to the church to ensure a bright display at their own funerals.

Because the fates of bees and humans were so linked, people believed that humans—especially beekeepers—could lure the prized insects away when they

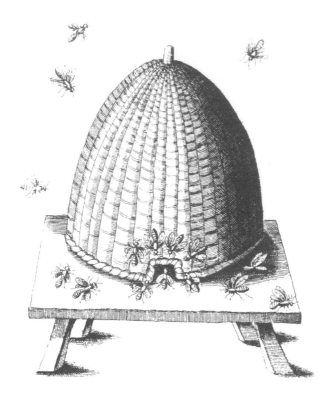

died. So survivors took the precaution of "telling" the bees when a death occurred in the family, perhaps to alert them to the change and earn their favor.

All the way up through the eighteenth century in rural England, a relative of the deceased might knock on a resident beehive or tie a crepe band around it before informing those inside of the loss, repeating the deceased's name with all due solemnity to caution the bees not to follow that person. To neglect the custom was to risk the bees abandoning their hives, never to return.

Other practices included the "heaving up" of the hives when the funeral party prepared to leave the house. Both hive and coffin would be "heaved" or lifted at the same moment. When the corpse of a beekeeper was carried from the house, any hives he tended were gingerly turned around so they wouldn't see the keeper pass and try to follow.

When sugar arrived on the scene, and bees and honey stopped being a key focus of community life, customs like these began to fade. But the folklore seems especially poignant in light of alarming news that millions of commercial honeybees in the United States—still critical to modern agriculture as pollinators of crops—died in the spring of 2007 from a mysterious condition known as colony collapse disorder, or "vanishing bee syndrome." All over America, large commercial beekeepers preparing for the spring pollinating season opened their hives to find the bees dead or missing altogether. Some reported losses of up to 95 percent, and at the time of this writing, no one is quite sure why. A mite infestation, pesticides, viruses, fungus, and stress are the prevailing theories.

See also: *Superstitions.*

BELL (TOLLING OF)

In Christian Europe but also in some Asian and tribal cultures, bells have long been linked with death. They both signaled the spirit to move on and drove away evil spirits that might seize the released soul or otherwise obstruct its journey.

In Britain as late as the reign of King Charles II in the seventeenth century, the soul or "passing" bell announced a death in the parish. Bell ringers used the number and pattern of strokes to relay the age, sex, and social status of the deceased, and were well paid for their pains. By the time

the poet John Donne composed the famous line "For whom the bell tolls," ringing of the soul bell in a recognizable pattern or knell was an established way of notifying the public about a death.
See also: *Appeasing the dead.*

BIER
The stand on which a corpse, coffin, or casket is carried or placed.

BIRDS
(AS SYMBOLS OF DEATH, THE SOUL, IMMORTALITY)
Birds haunt human superstitions, often signifying misfortune or prophecy. Like angels, they're creatures of air, not earthbound like humans. They're more spirit than body and can pass between worlds, bearing messages from beyond.

In Welsh folklore, a supernatural bird called Aderyne y Corph foretells a person's death, while in English lore, the cry of a whippoorwill near a house means one of its inhabitants will soon die. Likewise, a bird tapping at a window or flying inside a house is bad news.

In many mythologies, birds harbor the souls of the newly dead and to hear their call is to be summoned to the beyond. Seagulls are believed to be the souls of sailors, and when the title character in Samuel Taylor Coleridge's poem *The Rime of the Ancient Mariner* thoughtlessly kills an albatross his crew deems lucky, he brings a nightmarish curse upon the ship.

In Egypt, the *ba,* or soul, is depicted as a hawk with a human head. It was thought to exit at death and then, once the body was entombed, swoop and glide around the burial site at night. Egyptians left cakes to feed the *ba* and ensure it would not turn to and seek them out.

When asked where his soul resides, the ogre in an old Hindu tale replies, "Sixteen miles away is a tree. Surrounding the tree are tigers and bears and scorpions and snakes; on top is a great snake; on his head is a little cage; in the cage is a bird; my soul is in that bird."

The symbol for Techlotl, the Aztec god of the underworld, was a night owl, and the ancient Romans—unlike the Greeks, who valued the owl as the favored creature of Athena, goddess of wisdom—saw owls as evil. They ritually purified Rome if so much as a single owl strayed into the capital city.

Owls, magpies, ravens, and crows feature in many European traditions as bad omens, faring better in North American lore. In southwestern Arizona, Papago warriors who died were believed to turn into owls and assist living warriors in their struggles against the Apaches. "The medicine man sat on a little hill waiting for the owl-dead to come to him," a woman named Chona reported to the Columbia anthropologist who recorded her autobiography and published it as *Papago Woman* in 1936. "He had dreamed of owls himself so he could speak to them. They always took an Owl-Meeter on to war with them to call the dead who are our spies."

Carrion birds are very literally associated with death. Scavenger birds that subsist on the meat of dead animals are the tireless trash collectors of the Earth. Without them and animals like them, things would look and smell atrocious, but these birds don't get their due.

The Parsis, a Zoroastrian sect in India that traditionally forbids burial and cremation, leave their dead exposed to the elements. In Bombay in recent years, they had to stop placing them on the stone Towers of Silence when the vultures that once speedily dispatched the bodies began to mysteriously vanish. The decrease in vulture populations began in the early 1990s, with some 90 percent of two species of vulture—the white-backed and long-billed, formerly among India's most populous birds—left on the brink of extinction.

The vultures appear to be dying of acute kidney failure after consuming live-stock carcasses dosed with diclofenac, an anti-inflammatory used to ease fever.

See also: *Burial—air, Omens, Superstitions, Symbols.*

BODY SNATCHING

In ancient Rome dead babies were stolen and their parts used in recipes for witchcraft and sorcery. But the most grotesque chapter in the story of body snatching occurred long after science had put most ideas about witchcraft and sorcery to rest.

Until the late nineteenth century there was really no legal way for medical schools in Europe and the United States to get their scalpels on cadavers for anatomical study. So professional body snatchers stole them and sold them to the schools. Medical students and physicians also stole corpses for personal study.

Though Britain's Henry VIII approved a policy to donate the bodies of executed criminals to medical schools, demand still outweighed supply. Renaissance scientists rubbed elbows with dubious characters known as "resurrection men" while participating in a flourishing black market in bodies.

In Scotland, William Burke and William Hare ran a boardinghouse straight out of a modern horror movie. There they murdered hapless tenants and sold the remains to anatomy schools for up to ten pounds a corpse—nearly half a year's wages for the average workingman.

While Hare testified against his part-

ner in crime and was spared, Burke was eventually hanged and, in a macabre twist of justice, his body was publicly dissected. Sixteen murders were credited to these most infamous of resurrection men before the pair were convicted in Edinburgh in 1828.

By the mid-1830s, the United Kingdom and many U.S. states had passed the Anatomy Act, which ended the practice of using criminal corpses and allowing dissection when a person was too destitute to arrange for proper burial. This did next to no damage to the body trade and inspired the poor to protest.

More profitable than selling a corpse to the anatomical schools was the rarer practice of making off with a wealthy person's cadaver and holding it for ransom. In 1882, a man named Charles Souter was sentenced to five years for complicity in the removal of the body of the twenty-fifth earl of Crawford from the family vault near Aberdeen.

As recently as 1978, the body of comedian and film star Charlie Chaplin was briefly kidnapped from a Swiss cemetery by a pair of bungling thieves. In a bizarre plot twist that might have made for an entertaining silent movie, Chaplin's widow refused to produce the $600,000 ransom, saying her husband would have deemed the demand "ridiculous."

There has long been a trade in body parts as well. Someone in the Harcourt family purchased the heart of King Louis XIV of France from a grave robber during the French Revolution, storing the prize in a snuffbox. But one day he or someone in the household had the bad sense to display the heart for a visitor, the esteemed Dr. William Buckland, first professor of geology at Oxford University. Buckland had a taste for curious and exotic meat—from mole to crocodile—and when he saw the embalmed delicacy, he cried, "I have eaten many things, but never the heart of a king!" Before anyone could object, he partook.

In the contemporary Philippines, certain vigilante groups reportedly steal kneecaps from graves to hang around their necks as protection from enemy bullets.

See also: *Autopsy, Corpse, Forensic science.*

BON (OR *OBON*)

In Japan, memorial services may be held on the first anniversary of a death, then again after three, seven, thirteen, twenty-five, thirty-three, fifty, and even one hundred years. As in other places in Asia, memory and grief merge over the years into a more general respect for ancestors, but in mid-July or mid-August, depending on the region, the dead are believed to return to their old houses. Throughout the three-day festival called Bon, the living nourish, celebrate, and welcome them.

Souls arrive first at their final resting place, so families visit the family cemetery before the festival to tidy and decorate the tombs. The home is also cleaned and decorated with flowers and ornaments. Fires are lit with the smoke guiding the dead back home, where offerings of food and drink are set out for them on a family altar.

Bon is a time to visit friends and neighbors who have lately lost a loved one and bring gifts of food, money, lanterns, and incense. A priest may attend, reading prayers to aid the dead on their voyage to full enlightenment. Dances, called *bon odori*, are held to entertain the dead. In some regions, carrots and eggplants are carved into model horses so spirits can hitch a ride back to the other world when Bon is over.

For all the merriment, the first few anniversaries after the death of a loved one can be a painful time. After Bon, the dead go back to the other world, their way lit again by fires. In Nagasaki, they depart symbolically in large, specially built model boats, first as part of a happy, noisy parade in the street, then for their voyage out to sea.

See also: *Day(s) of the Dead, Funerary rites.*

BOOK OF THE DEAD– EGYPTIAN

A collection of spells and prayers usually written on a papyrus scroll and buried with dead Egyptians of the New Kingdom (1540–1075 BC). Intended as a manual for the afterlife, the text advised the dead person what to do and say when questioned about the life he or she had just left. Those who heeded these instructions and gave the right answers earned eternal life.

See also: *Hereafter.*

BOOK OF THE DEAD– TIBETAN

Commonly known in the West as the Tibetan Book of the Dead, a more literal translation might be "Liberation through understanding in the Between." This text helps Tibetan Buddhists reach final salvation and enlightenment.

After death but before rebirth, the soul navigates a mazelike "between" state called *bardo*. The text is read aloud to the dying and newly dead to guide the soul through this vast, at times confusing region to its optimal rebirth and eventually, if possible, to nirvana. Survivors pay a priest or lama to read to the wandering spirit, guiding it through and offering explicit instruction as needed.

See also: *Hereafter, Nirvana.*

BURIAL

A forty-five-foot-deep pit found in Atapuerca, Spain—filled with twenty-seven fossils of the hominid *Homo hedelbergensis*, an ancestor of Neanderthals and modern humans—suggests the practice of burying the dead is at least 350,000 years old.

While the Church of England's Book of Common Prayer helped "Earth to earth, ashes to ashes, dust to dust" become the staple phrase of Christian burial, the view predates the Bible and the written word.

The earliest burials were surely a way to shield the remains of the dead from scavengers. Later, people symbolically "planted" the dead to spur new life. All flesh originated from Mother Earth, so it made sense that the body—if not the spirit—should return there.

As communities grew, burial sites grew too. City cemeteries in Europe were especially overpopulated, and the dead were piled layer over layer. In the 1800s many urban graveyards ceased operation, with spacious parklike cemeteries springing up at the outskirts of cities and towns.

A conventional funeral arranged by a funeral director in the United States these days will set you back, on average, about seven thousand dollars.

Active involvement in the burial, such as throwing handfuls of dirt on the grave, is still common to many cultures, giving family and close friends the opportunity to participate in a formal, healing act of closure.

Humans are not the only species to enact burial. Elephants and chimps have been observed draping or heaping branches and leaves over their dead.

See also: *Barrow, Casket, Catacomb, Cemetery, Charnel house, Coffin, Funerary rites, Sarcophagus, Tomb.*

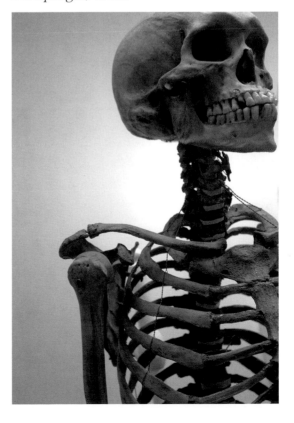

BURIAL-AIR

Many North American tribes, including the Crow Indians, used air "burial" or the practice of exposing a corpse by placing it in a tree or on a scaffold or high platform, to speed both decomposition and the soul's passage to the spirit world.

After the body dried in the wind for months or a year, a relative might come back for the remains and ready them for a second burial in the ground, or gingerly scrape remaining flesh from the bones, wash and dry them, and settle them in a "bone house" or ossuary.

Scaffold burial involved leaving the corpse on a scaffold in a tree or on a platform propped on poles dug firmly into the ground. Many eastern woodland and Great Lakes tribes, such as the Choctaw, Chickasaw, and Omaha, carefully wrapped their dead from head to foot in mats before laying them on platforms. For the Cheyenne, who ranged over the plains states of Missouri, Oklahoma, Kansas, and the Dakotas, baskets were a common method of transport and could also serve as burial platforms.

Today there are some 120,000 Parsis living and practicing in New Delhi, India. These followers of the ancient Persian religion Zoroastrianism hold earth, water, and fire sacred and believe these must have no contact with decaying flesh. They build large stone Towers of Silence on hills, leaving their dead out to be eaten by vultures. The exposed bones are allowed to bleach in the sun and are then moved into an ossuary pit or well at the center of the tower, where they might be treated with lime and allowed to disintegrate.

New Caledonians and people of the inland mountains of Borneo traditionally set their dead upright in the trunks of hollow trees, repositioning the bark over the corpse to hide it from predators, while in New Zealand, the Maoris placed dead bodies on branches or in the hollow trunk of a tree as part of their ceremony called *tangi,* meaning "to cry." Other traditional peoples in New Zealand might lay exhumed bones in a hollowed tree or on a platform in trees as the secondary burial.

See also: *Birds, Funerary rites.*

BURIAL-AT A CROSSROADS

Ancient Teutonic people constructed altars and carried out ritual human sacrifice at crossroads, so these spots came to be thought of as execution grounds. Later, Christians adapted these dark associations to the long-standing idea that some corpses were more likely to revive and "walk" than others. Criminals, suicides, and other "dangerous" dead might be buried in the dark of night at a crossroads and marked only by a crude cross, the idea being that they would be too confused to find their way home or wreak havoc on their one-time associates.

Speakers' Corner, situated in the northeast corner of London's Hyde Park where two ancient Roman roads once intersected, was formerly the home of the Tyburn hanging tree. The first recorded execution there took place in 1196, though the site may have been an established crossroads execution ground as early as 1108. Today a stone plaque on a traffic island near Marble Arch marks the place where the gallows once stood.

See also: *Appeasing the dead, Funerary rites.*

BURIAL—ECO (OR *GREEN*)

Burials in America deposit 827,060 gallons of embalming fluid (formaldehyde, methanol, and ethanol) into the soil each year, and with so many people living "greener," more environmentally conscious lives, many are arranging for greener deaths as well.

A Swedish company can freeze-dry your body in liquid nitrogen, pulverize the brittle corpse with high-frequency vibrations, and seal the powdery result in a cornstarch coffin to be deterred in a shallow grave. Decomposition time? Six to twelve months.

In Australia, meanwhile, eco-friendly coffins made of wood fiber—90 percent of it derived from recycled materials—and bonded with natural glue are on offer.

In the United States, Ramsey Creek Preserve in South Carolina boasts the first (contemporary) green cemetery. Bodies are buried in their natural state without embalming, upright tombstones, or fancy caskets, wrapped in just a shroud or a family quilt, and planted over with wildflowers. Back to the earth—in record time!

See also: *Burial—water, Funerary rites, Natural death movement.*

BURIAL-IN CHURCH

It was common practice before the eighteenth century to bury the dead in church. Whole church floors were paved with individual tombstones, with the structure literally rising out of a cemetery.

BURIAL-PREMATURE

Pliny wrote of Romans waking on their own flaming funeral pyres after being wrongly pronounced dead. "Such is the condition of humanity," he concluded, "and so uncertain is men's judgment, that they cannot determine even death itself."

In the Middle Ages, crude tests of death included holding a candle near the mouth of a person presumed dead, since breath would cause the flame to flicker, or using a feather or mirror to the same end. Fear of a live burial made medieval funerals long, elaborate affairs.

Legends of thieves or rogue gravediggers waking the dead when they set out to steal their jewelry flourished during the Renaissance, as did stories of people rising up en route to a funeral or even later in the grave. By the time of Edgar Allan Poe—who explored the theme often in his fiction—sensational tales of being buried alive filled medical journals, newspapers, and popular magazines. When graves were exhumed in such instances, witnesses found ripped and bloody shrouds, broken limbs and battered foreheads, missing fingers and chewed shrouds. Underground groans sounded from graves, and in one notably grisly tale, a young Swedish woman, who had perished in a state of advanced pregnancy, was exhumed in a local churchyard only to find she had given birth to a child in her coffin.

The number of exhumed skeletons reportedly found in ghastly, contorted poses in their coffins in the eighteenth and nineteenth centuries led to speculation that *one in ten* bodies was being planted six feet under before the person was even dead.

How did such horrific "accidents" happen? There are many possible explanations: fainting, concussion, asphyxia or lack of oxygen, trances, narcotic overdose (not least in Victorian times, when apothecaries blithely prescribed "poppy water" cordials), but historically the terror of premature burial has spawned its own rituals and peculiar safeguards.

The Romans cried out a person's name three times before laying the body on the pyre. Hebrew tradition called for storing it in a cave or open sepulchre and regularly checking for a time. Some people waited for decay to set in before they buried or cremated a body.

In times of plague—as in Marseilles between 1720 and 1722, when half the city's population was lost and the streets were littered with corpses—the infected were often in the ground within a few hours. Mass graves were common, and despite the habit of driving a long bronze pin deliberately under the big toenail to test for signs of life, many individuals were no doubt buried alive.

The eighteenth-century Danish anatomist Jacques-Bénigne Winslow said the absence of respiratory activity or a pulse didn't guarantee that death had occurred. The only sure signs were the onset of putrefaction and telltale "livid spots." None thought the lifeless should be swiftly shrouded and interred. Leave them in a warm bed, Winslow advised, and try resuscitating first. Irritate their nostrils with the juice of onions and horseradish; pour vinegar and pepper into their mouths; tickle them with the quill of a pen, press them with nettles, slice the soles of their feet with razors, or thrust a pointed pencil up their unfortunate noses.

Ghastly though these methods seem, they were humanitarian at heart. Were many saved from untimely demise by having a pin pried under the toenail? Tough to say, but in the nineteenth century public fear of premature burial inspired innovations like security coffins and waiting mortuaries for decaying corpses.

In 1896, in England, the Association for the Prevention of Premature Burial was formed for people who wanted scientific tests performed on their corpses before they were buried.
See also: *Security coffins, Signs of death, Waiting mortuaries.*

BURIAL–SECOND
(OR *DOUBLE*)
Many traditions hold that a corpse is not really "dead" until the flesh is off the bones—the body is considered neither alive nor fully in the spirit world. Until this "second death," often several years after the fact when the body is exhumed and the bones gathered up, cleaned, and transferred to a final resting place, such as the family tomb, a corpse is considered dangerous.

In Greece a body may be exhumed one to three years after burial, when the flesh has disintegrated. Loved ones might open the grave, hold up a skull, kiss and cry for it, and pass it to each relative in turn. Between the first and second burials, while the corpse is in the earth, mourning women might visit the village cemetery in the evening to weed and tidy the tomb, pass the time with neighbors, or reflect on the departed.

In Madagascar, the body is exhumed and the bones washed. Before returning them to the tomb, relatives may take the deceased to a place or event that he or she enjoyed during life—a dance, a festival, a soccer game. Then the bones are carefully replaced in the tomb, finally coming to rest in the ancestor world.
See also: *Appeasing the dead, Mourning.*

BURIAL–WATER
The theme of "crossing over" to the other world, of death as a journey over water, pervades human myth and folklore. Not surprisingly, island inhabitants, seafaring cultures, and other societies with practical ties to the ocean and rivers also incorporate water and boats into their death rites.

In the lore of sailors, a corpse on board spells misfortune and must be swiftly

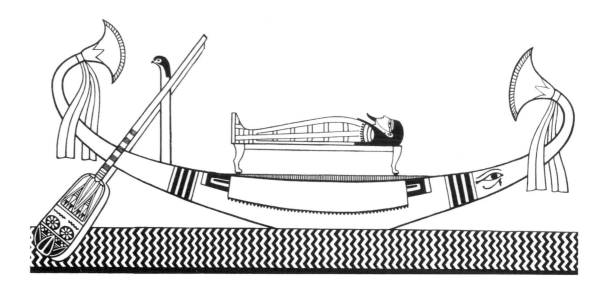

buried at sea, dropped feet first into the waves lest it bring bad luck or bad weather.

Many cultures incorporated a ship or boat literally into the funeral proceedings. Entire ships heaped with items have been found at ancient Egyptian burial sites. Scandinavians also buried whole boats with heroes decked out in full regalia, seated upright and encircled by gifts and human and animal sacrifices. They might also launch the equipped ship and its dead voyager out to sea.

Sometimes a boat and its inhabitants were cremated with only rivets in the grave revealing that a ship burial had taken place.

Some Native Americans also used boats in funerary customs. Northwest coastal tribes like the Chinook of Washington often conducted canoe-platform burials, treating the crafts as coffins with symbolic meaning. While commoners were simply thrown into the sea, some-times with weights, the use of a canoe as a coffin—once common in Hawaii, Tahiti, and New Zealand as well, if mostly reserved for chieftains—is still reported in Samoa and Fiji.

Burial at sea is still a popular form of disposition for the U.S. Navy. According to Environmental Protection Agency guidelines, "burial at sea of human remains that are not cremated shall take place at least three nautical miles from land and in water at least 600 feet deep."

Green burial methods are flourishing at sea as well as on land. One company has developed biodegradable urns shaped like giant seashells the size of toilet lids; when tossed in the water, they float awhile before sinking, and eventually dissolve. A U.S. company called Eternal Reefs entrusts human remains to a module that mimics a coral reef. The reef balls, which last five hundred years, are then dropped into the ocean to create new marine habitats.

See also: *Burial—eco.*

CAPITAL PUNISHMENT
(OR *DEATH PENALTY*)

The sentence of punishment by execution is one of the most ancient rights exercised by the state. When the rulers of Babylonia had their laws carved on stone columns four thousand or so years ago, the death penalty was among them.

Most societies have instituted capital punishment at some point, though not for the same crimes. The fate is generally reserved for egregious offenses like murder and treason, but some have succumbed for stealing a loaf of bread or poking fun at a ruler.

Today, the goal—though not always met—is swift and painless execution; in the past, executions were purposefully cruel and horrifying. In thirteenth-century England, a person accused of being a traitor might be hanged, drawn and quartered, beheaded, disemboweled, *and* burned. Any one of these methods would have sufficed, of course, but the execution was not only a punishment; it was a public statement (and usually these proceedings *were* public, a spectacle attended in droves) meant to discourage others from treasonous activities, an idea that persisted in many places until reforms began in earnest in the nineteenth century.

The practice of hanging or displaying the remains of executed criminals, known as gibbeting, kept the warning present, even after the fact. In an extreme example of extending the message, an 1832 account of the crime and dissection of executed British murderer John Horwood was bound in the killer's own tanned skin.

Named after Dr. Joseph Ignace Guillotin, who did not invent it but lobbied for its use, France's guillotine was designed to be a humane alternative to hanging. But the "national razor" caused controversy when a well-known anatomist asked in a 1795 editorial in the Paris *Moniteur*: "Don't you know that the seat of the feelings and appreciation is in the brain, that this seat of consciousness can continue to operate even when the circulation of the blood is cut off from the brain?" As long as the brain retained its vital force, he

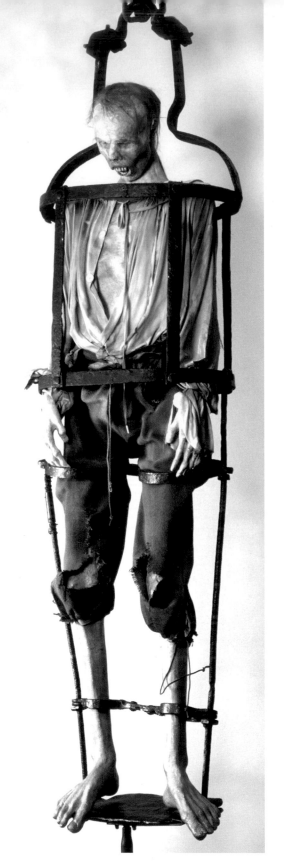

The gibbet, a device used for the public exhibition of the bodies of criminals and traitors after execution.

argued, the victim was conscious. Heads, lopped from the shoulders of men, had been known to grimace and grind their teeth. "The guillotine is terrible torture!" he urged, advising further testing and experimentation. "We must return to hanging."

Not long after, in an interview, a Paris executioner's assistant claimed to have witnessed only immediate death at time of impact, which eased the public's mind a bit.

Capital punishment is still controversial today. Even in a modern, humane climate, methods aren't foolproof. Over the past hundred years, U.S. states have selected from and discarded as many as five execution techniques, including the noose and the electric chair. Lethal injection, the latest effort to "find a way to transport condemned inmates from life to death in a manner that does not offend our civilized sensibilities," noted Elizabeth Weil in a 2007 article in the *New York Times Magazine,* "are often botched and sometimes painful." She reported that "the American Veterinary Medical Association issues and reviews recommendations for euthanizing animals. No one in the United States does anything similar for condemned inmates."

CASKET

A casket is a more recent and, as a rule, more luxurious version of a coffin.
See also: *Burial, Coffin, Sarcophagus.*

CATACOMB

A network of underground rooms and corridors used as a burial place, catacombs have graves cut into the walls. In Rome and Sicily, the mummified bodies of monks and others could be preserved this way for centuries as a spectacle for visitors.

One of the world's most famous catacombs is the "empire of the dead" in Paris, a network of subterranean tunnels and rooms in depleted Roman-era limestone quarries. In 1786, burial conditions in area cemeteries had become unsanitary, spreading disease, so Paris authorities quietly relocated the bones to the tunnels.

To brave the myriad dim passageways today is to encounter the remains of millions of former Parisians. Bones—methodically fitted together, with skulls punctuating at intervals—line the walls. The remains are labeled by year of burial.

Public access is officially restricted, with illegal entry punishable by a fine, but people still find their way in through sewers, manholes, and the Metro subway system. During World War II, some Parisian cells of the French resistance used the tunnel system, but today the catacombs are a known site for altogether different furtive liaisons: drug dealers and users, eccentrics, and urban explorers known as "cataphiles" may spend days at a time underground. Tours are given on a limited basis.
See also: *Charnel house, Tomb.*

CAUSE OF DEATH

Causes of death range among three major categories: degeneration, or biological deterioration of the body as with heart disease, cancer, or stroke; communicable or infectious diseases, such as tuberculosis, pneumonia, and malaria; and deaths attributed to the social and economic environment, including suicide and fatal accidents. These categories overlap, of course: a person might die of cancer related to asbestos in the workplace, for instance. Age, sex, and race are all factors.

Right now the two major causes of death in most Western countries are circulatory system diseases (including heart attacks and strokes) and cancers. No American has died of old age since 1951, the year the government did away with that classification on death certificates. Lack of oxygen always triggers death, and its decrease can cause muscle spasms, bringing on the "agonal phase," from the Greek word *agon,* or contest.
See also: *Autopsy, Burial—premature, Forensic science.*

CEMETERY (OR *GRAVEYARD*)

Early Christian writers came up with the word "cemetery," derived from the Greek word *koimeterion,* meaning "to sleep," to describe a burial site in the earth.

Cemeteries in ancient times were most often situated outside of towns, along the roads, but as villages and communities grew and churches were built, grave-

and a tick list of departed celebrities. Tourists and sightseers came on outings or for picnics bearing guidebooks.

Paris's Pere-Lachaise was among the first modern cemeteries, and Brookwood Cemetery, built by the London Necropolis Company ("necropolis" is a Greek word meaning "city of the dead," and it's what scholars call cemeteries in ancient cities), was one of the largest. Thirty miles outside London, Brookwood boasted a private railway station in the city and its own train line with a station sign that read NECROPOLIS.

What is now called the Mount Auburn Cemetery in Cambridge, Massachusetts, was the first rural or "garden" cemetery in America, built 176 years ago, a model for others that sprang up in Hartford, Chicago, and San Francisco, and for the public parks generally. Mount Auburn rests on 175 beautifully landscaped acres

yards were incorporated or added. Early on, the prestigious dead might be buried inside the church: VIPs under the altar; the minister under the pulpit; the otherwise distinguished under the floor of the nave or aisles. As local populations grew, burial space spilled out to an adjoining churchyard.

City graveyards, especially in Europe, at last became so overcrowded that the dead had to be stacked or the plots reused; remains were exhumed after a given period of time, and the bones were shifted to a charnel or catacomb, making graves available for fresh corpses.

In the 1800s, many crowded urban graveyards were closed and new parklike ones were built outside of cities and towns. The first modern cemeteries were as much retreats for urbanites as burial places for the dead, featuring pastoral settings, sculptures and monuments crafted by famous artists and architects,

of winding paths and ponds, and showcases five thousand trees representing 630 taxa. A museum, National Historic Landmark dedicated to preservation and conservation, and botanic garden, it remains an active cemetery. Some 200,000 people visit annually—from mourners to birdwatchers—to stroll, meditate, and study the historic collection of architecture and memorials, representing the nineteenth through the twenty-first centuries.

Today there are more than 150,000 burial sites in the United States from small family plots to church graveyards to huge urban and military cemeteries. See also: *Burial, Catacombs, Charnel house.*

CEMETERY–PET

Often the first experience we have of death, as children, is the loss of a com-

panion animal. Many of us accept dogs, cats, and other animals into our families and sorely grieve them when they die. Pet cemeteries, whether actual or virtual, let us memorialize them. "Online" pet cemeteries allow people to post photos—with links serving as "plots"—and epitaphs by way of honoring them and sharing our memories with others.

CHARNEL HOUSE

Charnel houses were medieval structures that surrounded a cemetery. The bones removed from older graves were stored there, allowing fresh corpses to take their place.
See also: *Catacomb, Cemetery.*

CHEATING DEATH

In W. Somerset Maugham's retelling of an Arabian folk story, Death narrates her conversation with a merchant in Baghdad. Earlier in the day, the merchant's servant had encountered and been frightened by Death in the marketplace. He raced home and pleaded for his master's horse so that he might ride to nearby Samarra and elude her advances. The merchant loans the servant this horse, and away he gallops. Later at the market, the merchant himself bumps into Death, inquiring why she had looked at his poor servant in so threatening a way. Death explains that it was just a start of surprise. "I was astonished to see him in Baghdad," she says. "For I had an appointment with him tonight in Samarra."

From this compact story, with its wicked irony, to the horror film series *Final Destination,* in which a group of students who "cheat death" by avoiding a plane crash must eventually succumb, one by one, in grisly fashion, world folklore, literature, and popular culture are replete with tales of people trying, and invariably failing, to outwit an ever implacable and entitled Death.

See also: *Dance of death, Death (personified).*

COFFIN

This word comes from the Greek word for "basket," and until relatively recent times a basket or basketlike chest might be used for almost anything *but* a corpse, from jewelry to herbs and spices. Coffins are traditional wedge-shape boxes or receptacles, made usually of lead or wood, in which a dead body is buried or cremated. They vary in shape, size, and color worldwide.

Polish coffins of the eighteenth century were sometimes decorated with painted portraits of the deceased; tribesmen of Ecuador painted the coffin of a child white, using magenta or orange for that of an adult; and in Victorian England, coffins were sometimes elaborately carved. But more often, coffins were plain and practical. The stark wooden box, narrow at head and feet and wide at shoulders, was in general use for many centuries, and traditional Amish still use such a box, handcrafted after the corpse has been measured with string or a stick.

Mahogany and heavy-gauged metal, copper, or brass coffins or caskets designed to be lowered into waterproof cement vaults have come into wide use only in modern times.

Millionaire Sandra West of San Antonio, Texas, who died in 1977, chose a real status symbol as her coffin. She was buried in her nightgown, sitting in the front seat of her beloved blue Ferrari. To deter grave robbers, the car was encased in concrete.

See also: *Burial, Casket, Sarcophagus.*

COFFIN-SECURITY

Fear of premature burial had people in the seventeenth, eighteenth, and nineteenth centuries requesting to be buried with axes, spades, and trumpets, and inspired a host of novel inventions over the years, not least the security coffin.

In the 1790s, a German duke commissioned a specimen with a window that let light in, an air hole to prevent suffocation, and a lid that wasn't nailed down but employed a lock-and-key mechanism (he'd keep a key to both coffin and aboveground crypt in a special pocket stitched into his shroud).

Christian Eisenbrandt of Baltimore was granted a patent in 1843 for a "new and useful improvement in coffins." His was rigged so the lid would spring open if the occupant shifted even slightly. It only worked aboveground.

On offer in England was the Bateson Life Revival Device, patented in 1852, an iron bell mounted on the lid of the casket with its rope connecting to the resident's hand through a hole in the lid. Known as Bateson's Belfry, this method was likewise more useful before burial than after.

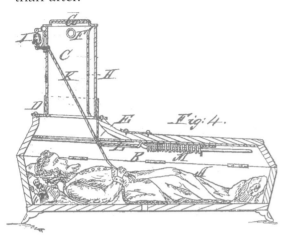

A Belgian model connected a tube from the coffin to the ground's surface with a box holding a flag, bell, and lamp positioned over the outside end of the tube. Any movement of the chest of the interred would activate a spring-loaded ball, at which point the box lid opened to admit light and air into the coffin, the flag appeared, the lamp blazed, and the bell rang. (Interestingly enough, this is not where we get the expression "saved by the bell," which is a boxing term from the 1930s.)

In the United States, at least twenty-two patent applications for security coffins were submitted between 1868 and 1925. In some cases, electrical signals triggered flags, bells, and rotating lights; the most elaborate even employed electric light, heating, and a telephone.

The sad fact is that a living person shut in the average coffin with the lid screwed down would expire in an hour for lack of oxygen. So unless you woke promptly, you were out of luck.

CONSCIOUSNESS (OF DEATH)

"The human race is the only one that knows it must die," wrote the philosopher Voltaire, "and it knows this only through its experience. A child brought up alone and transported to a desert island would have no more idea of death than a bird or a plant."

Is it a blessing or a curse—to know?

Though humankind has owned this knowledge since the beginning of recorded time, we have all manner of ways of processing it. Death has changed over the centuries just as human life has changed.

In his book *The Hour of Our Death*, Philippe Aries tracks those changes, arguing that for the ancient Greeks and Romans on through the first ten centuries of the Christian era, death—both for heroes and for ordinary people—was

WHERE IS THE CURE?

Stricken with grief, a woman wandered everywhere with her dead child in her arms in search of a cure. Finally she came to Buddha, who said he might heal the child on only one condition: "Go and beg a handful of poppy seeds from a home that death has never entered."

After searching in vain for such a house, she returned to Buddha in defeat. In his quiet presence her mind cleared, the story goes, and she understood the meaning of his words. She took the body away and buried it, and then returned to Buddha and became one of his followers.

too familiar to be terrifying. It was accepted and announced in relation to the community as a whole, the dominant concern. The community, in turn, paid its respects and rallied anew.

Only in the eleventh century, Aries says, did the individual begin to seem paramount. Death was no longer a temporary weakening of the community but a personal threat, the end of the self. This, together with new Christian ideas about the Last Judgment and fear of the afterlife, made the idea of a "better life in the hereafter" feel increasingly important.

In the sixteenth century, the focus shifted from attention to death of self to death of another. As family began to displace community more and more, the theme of passionate attachment to lover, child, and spouse increasingly made the separation feel unbearable, and a mood of wild grief prevailed.

Death in the nineteenth century, meanwhile, was the prerequisite for reunion in the next world, and mourning and consolation were elevated to a socially demanding art form.

In our own time, in Western society, death is something to look staunchly away from, to banish altogether from our daily lives; it is a private terror, hidden in plain sight.

In contrast, from its inception, Buddhism has stressed the importance of death. Teachers advise students toward a mindfulness of death. Life is impermanence, and everyone who has ever lived has died.

So human consciousness of death can take many turns—from open acceptance to outright denial.

See also: *Euphemism, Thanatology.*

CORPSE (OR *BODY, CADAVER*)

The unfortunate truth is that our dead bodies aren't much use to us or to anyone we love. It's all about disposal from there on in, usually burial or cremation, unless you've opted to donate your body to science, in which case what remains may be put to any number of good uses.

Without the anatomical understanding of the human body afforded by dissection, much of modern medicine wouldn't exist. As Mary Roach points out in *Stiff: The Curious Lives of Human Cadavers,* "For every new surgical procedure, from heart transplants to gender reassignment surgery, cadavers have been there, making history in their quiet, sundered way." One of the ways she cites is to act as a crash-test dummy. "To calibrate a crash-test dummy," Roach says, "you first need to know how much of an impact each real body part can take. To find out, researchers in the 1960s—and to a lesser extent today—subjected carefully instrumented cadavers to simulated crashes and blows. The contributions of the dead are nothing short of heroic: For every cadaver used to test and develop airbags, for example, 147 lives are saved." What Roach calls the "ghastly, necessary science of impact tolerance," with dead bodies enduring all the horrific, wrenching things that can happen to a live body in a car crash, allows automobile manufacturers to design safer cars. A simulated dummy can give a guess at what a real body can or can't take and at what speed, but it takes a real body to prove it.

Is there such a thing as a too-useful corpse? The English philosopher Jeremy Bentham, who died in 1832, left his body to University College of London, asking that it be dissected, stuffed, and displayed for posterity. Evidently it's still

there, decked out in his favorite clothes and sporting a straw hat and walking stick, 175 years after his death.

See also: *Autopsy, Forensic science, Organ donorship.*

CREMATION

The practice of disposing of a body by burning it to ashes has been around for thousands of years, from the ancient Romans, who cremated their dead, storing the ashes in decorative urns, to the Tlingit Indians, who cremated theirs to offer warmth for the arduous journey to the spirit world.

Archeological findings in Scandinavia suggest that some early northern Europeans burned the wings of crows and jackdaws on the pyre with the body, perhaps to symbolically bear the soul aloft.

Many cultures think of fire as "the blazing servant of God," equipped to free spirit from body and fly it into the next life.

The Dani people of Papua anoint the body with fat from a freshly slaughtered pig before resting it on the funeral pyre, over which a kinsman holds a bundle of grass while another shoots the grass with an arrow, instantly releasing the spirit of the deceased.

Hindus, for whom cremation is more or less universal, see the body as an offering to Agni, the Fire God. For centuries the banks of the Ganges River have housed burning *ghats*—today often commercially operated marble or concrete slabs at the river's edge. A body is wrapped in cloth and set on or within a pile of wood, and a Hindu's eldest son is charged with lighting the fire. Melted butter called *ghee* is thrown on the flames to help the body burn. In three days the ashes are gathered up, bound in cloth, and laid in the river.

To pilgrims seeking spiritual cleansing, water purified by the souls of the dead and dense with human ashes is deeply holy. Hindus in other countries may ask to have their ashes mailed back to India.

For the Balinese, liberation precludes reincarnation, so a cremation ceremony is often a joyful affair. But all must be suitably arranged before the pyre is lit. Custom demands an elaborate coffin and cremation tower, a lavish feast for mourners and guests, and other meticulous and expensive preparations. It may take years to save enough money to do

things right, during which the body is temporarily buried.

Many North Americans now choose to be cremated for personal or environmental reasons (cremation conserves land), and families scatter the ashes somewhere that meant something to the deceased, for instance, in a garden, a body of water, or a wilderness area. They may also keep the ashes of loved ones in special urns.

On April 21, 1997, the remains of *Star Trek* series creator Gene Roddenberry were launched into outer space together with those of twenty-four others by a company called Celestis.

Modern cremation can pump dioxins, hydrochloric acid, sulfur dioxide, and carbon dioxide into the air, as well as mercury, a toxic metal used for dental fillings that causes severe pollution when vaporized; as a result, many crematoriums are researching filters to reduce "emissions."

See also: *Burial—eco, Funerary rites, Mementos, Pyre.*

CRYONICS

In 1964 a Michigan physics teacher named Robert Ettinger published a book called *The Prospect of Immortality,* inspired by a sci-fi story and by the theory that living people could be revived after freezing, should the technology to perform cellular repairs be developed in the future. Within a few years, an international movement was under way. The Cryonics Society of Michigan, later the Cryonics Association, was formed in 1967. Today there are similar societies in Canada, Germany, Australia, Japan, and many other countries.

Cryonics is a medical procedure and scientific experiment that involves freezing a body at extremely low temperatures in the hopes of preserving the body tissue indefinitely until cellular repairs are possible.

Immediately after death, the blood is removed and substituted with a fluid similar to that used to preserve organs for transplant. After surgery, the body is slowly lowered into a large container of liquid nitrogen at sub-300 degrees Fahrenheit.

The first person to enter cryonic suspension was James Bedford, who died of cancer in 1967. His frozen body is stored at the Alcor Life Extension Foundation, near Phoenix, Arizona. By 2001, the number of people cryopreserved at Alcor was about eighty. Several cats and dogs have been preserved as well, by people intent on a future reunion with their pets.

This "bigfoot" Dewar is custom designed to contain four whole-body patients and six neuro-patients immersed in liquid nitrogen at −196 degrees Celsius. The Dewar is an insulated container that consumes no electric power. Liquid nitrogen is added periodically to replace the small amount that evaporates.

Alcor began using vitrification in 2000, a protocol that greatly reduces the formation of ice crystals during the cryopreservation process. About 65 percent of Alcor's patients have had only their heads preserved, because they believe the brain houses their memories and identity and is therefore most important to cryopreserve. Alcor's most famous patient, Hall of Fame slugger Ted Williams, had both his head and torso cryo-preserved.

Today, Alcor can partially vitrify the body, but is still researching how to fully vitrify all of the body's tissues simultaneously. The cost of cryopreservation is affordable for most people using a life insurance policy that names the cryonics provider as the beneficiary. The cost of cryopreservation at the Alcor Foundation at the time of this writing was $80,000 for neuropreservation and $150,000 for whole-body cryopreservation. The cost of the life insurance policy varies depending on a person's health and age. Other funding options include trusts, annuities, and prepaid cash "or equivalent."

See also: *Eternal life (quest for)*.

CRYPT

A chamber or vault with an arched or domed ceiling in which a body is placed. From the Latin word *crypta,* adapted from Greek, for "hidden" or "concealed"—and later the vault in which valuables were stowed—burial crypts were at least partially underground. Historically, they were built under the main floor of a church.

From the time of the Norman Conquest on, Britain had few breaks from war or the threat of war. The constant threat of invasion or insurrection meant that a body buried in an unguarded cemetery might be dug up or defiled. So cathedrals and churches were often designed with the main floor covering and protecting with stone an underground burial place.

Now a crypt is more likely to be outside the walls of a church than under its floor. The drawers that hold bodies in mausoleums are often referred to as crypts.

See also: *Burial, Catacombs, Tomb.*

DANCE OF DEATH
(OR DANSE MACABRE)

In the late Middle Ages, as the Black Death decimated the populations of Europe, the wages of sin were high on everyone's mind, and church walls were ornamented with art warning sinners to repent before death came for them.

In images of the *danse macabre,* or dance of death, smirking, skeletal Death, animated and usually wearing a crown, leads kings and beggars, laborers and ladies, doctors and monks in a stunned procession to their demise. Everyone dies, was the message, regardless of wealth or status, and this theme—death as the great equalizer—appealed to writers and artists. The motif became central to art, music, poetry, and literature of the age, in everything from ballads and dramatic pageants to tapestries and stained glass.

In Holbein's famous graphic version, printed in 1538, Death scoops up a miser's gold, snatches a child from the family hearth, scales a sailor's mast, and jousts with a knight.

See also: *Memento mori, Plague.*

DAY(S) OF THE DEAD

As October gives way to November, the Mexican festival of Todos Santos, or All Saints'—a blending of the Christian feasts of All Saints' and All Souls'—takes place. Commonly called Dia or Dia de Muertos (Day, or Day of the Dead), it's the time of year when the spirits of the dead drop by for a visit, returning from a world much like this one to partake again of the pleasures they knew in life.

In Mexico the worlds of the living and the dead coexist in a constant state of interaction. Day of the Dead combines Aztec beliefs about the importance of death with the Catholic feast, but it's really a family event, a joyful reunion. So while there's a public aspect with fireworks and bustling markets hawking candy sugar skulls, toy coffins, and traditional paper puppets, the heart of the event happens in the home.

The souls of children, or *angelitos,* little angels, return first—on October 30 and 31—and food and gifts for them are set out early. When the children withdraw, offerings are made to adult souls on November 1. The blue smoke of burning *copal* incense leads them home, where flowers, food, and drink are laid out in welcome on candlelit tables. People decorate *ofrendas,* or home altars, with photos of dead relatives, crepe paper flowers or real marigolds, and palm leaves. Similar items are laid out later on tombs.

In rural areas, preparation and anticipation take place throughout the year.

In larger towns and urban settings like Mexico City, public celebrations can be exuberant and funny and attract swarms of tourists. Museums and galleries exhibit artistic *ofrendas,* and in the streets, people jeer at Death and befriend it. A profusion of skeletons mimics the living, each posed and outfitted for ordinary activity—you might stumble across sequined discos for the dead, for instance, with strobe lights whirling.

See also: *Bon, Halloween.*

DEATH (PERSONIFIED)
The earliest recorded ideas about Death as an actual figure or messenger come from ancient Egypt and Mesopotamia. Egypt's jackal-headed god Anubis, who acted as the psycho pomp—a Greek word for "guide of souls"—is one early example.

Homer referred to death alternately as a winged harpy that snatched up her victims or as Thanatos, a winged youth with a sword.

Even today we have a vague sense of an "angel of death," that figure who walks over your grave—a distant grave in a distant future, of course—when we feel that dreaded "shudder." Many people still leave the window open in a room where someone has died so the spirit can depart in the company of the angel without incident.

In the Middle Ages, death was commonly represented as an animated skeleton, what has since become known as the Grim Reaper. In Brittany, Ankow summons the souls of those who are about to die. The last to die annually in a parish becomes the new "Ankow" for the year to come.

Recent young adult novels like Markus Zusak's *The Book Thief* and Martine Leavitt's' *Keturah and Lord Death* have put their own unique spin on the figure of Death, while in Neil Gaiman's classic *Sandman* series of graphic novels, Death is a Goth girl.

Whether a select god, a fearsome angel, a noble lord, or a grinning, implacable skeleton, one thing is sure: there is next to no bargaining with him or (more rarely) her. In Iranian myth, Zurvan, the time diety, held the honor. In popular depictions, both Father Time and the Grim Reaper carry a scythe, and either way the message is clear.

Every now and then a more positive spin on the harbinger-of-death theme occurs.

Keeping companion pets in nursing homes is a rising trend, but Oscar—feline mascot in an advanced-care unit at Steere House Nursing and Rehabilitation Center in Providence, Rhode Island—is in a category all his own. A cat with what Dr. David Dosa calls "an uncanny ability to predict when residents are about to die," Oscar has effectively announced the demise of more than twenty-five patients suffering final stages of Alzheimer's, Parkinson's, stroke, and other mentally debilitating diseases.

According to nursing staff, when Oscar pauses in his customary (and otherwise "aloof") rounds and settles on a bed to snuggle and purr, it's time to summon the patient's family. Usually the bed's inhabitant has less than four hours to live. "[Oscar] doesn't make too many mistakes," says Dosa, a geriatrician and assistant professor of medicine at Brown University who wrote an article about Oscar for the *New England Journal of Medicine.* "He seems to understand when patients are about to die."

No one can say why, exactly, though it's been suggested that Oscar detects subtle changes in the metabolism or mental aura of a dying person. Or he may be just an unusually empathetic cat. Whatever the reason, many families value his vigils, says Dosa, and "appreciate the companionship that the cat provides for their dying loved one."

Hanging over the entrance to the Steere House dementia unit is a plaque that reads, "For his compassionate hospice care, this plaque is awarded to Oscar the Cat."
See also: *Angel of Death, Cheating death, Dance of death.*

DEATHBED PORTRAITS
In the nineteenth century and before—until photography made it possible for anyone to have a likeness of their loved ones—a family might commission a painter to memorialize a person just before or after he died. The dead were often painted as if they were still alive, especially children. A child could sicken and die within days, leaving a family with no means of recalling the way she looked or her special traits or "aspect." Artists incorporated symbols like broken-stemmed flowers in a nearby vase to hint that the likeness was in fact a deathbed interpretation. In colonial Mexico, nuns might have paintings done after death that depicted them in the habit and crown of flowers they first wore as "brides of Christ."
See also: *Death masks, Mementos, Postmortem photography.*

DEATH BRIDE (OR GROOM)
Because farmers in Transylvanian Romania consider *Stragoli,* or unfulfilled souls, the most restless of spirits, young unmarried men or women may be honored with a *nunta mortului,* or wedding of the dead, at their funeral—complete with fully attired bridesmaids and groomsmen.

If the deceased is an unmarried man, community woodsmen take to the forest and fetch a tall fir tree. They alternate ax blows, with no one male taking more than a single stroke, then haul the tree into the village, where women and girls greet the procession with song, dress the symbolic bride, and decorate it with ribbons. The singing continues all the way to the cemetery, with folk lyrics consoling the forlorn spirit and offering the tree as stand-in bride while its trunk is planted at the head of the grave.

For an unmarried girl, a young man from the village might stand by her coffin and speak vows before a priest. A doll representing the children the dead bride will never have is nestled by her side.

Posthumous weddings occur in other regions as well. Some Asian cultures honor such marriages, likewise believing that the spirits of the dead cannot rest until unfinished business—such as an intended ceremony—is completed.

A French law drafted during World War I on behalf of the fiancées of servicemen who died in the trenches was extended to civilians in December 1959. When the Malpasset Dam in southern France burst, claiming hundreds of lives, President Charles de Gaulle answered a woman's plea to allow her to follow through on her marriage plans even though her betrothed had died. Parliament drafted a law permitting Irene Jodard to marry her deceased fiancé. Since then, hundreds have applied for postmortem matrimony in France.

See also: *Appeasing the dead, Funerary rites.*

DEATH MASKS

Often made of gold, Egyptian death masks were crafted to represent the model, but that wasn't the case in all societies. When archeologist Alberto Ruz Lhuillier compared a jade-and-stucco mask from the corpse of a dead Mayan ruler to wall carvings of the man, the mask bore no resemblance to his face in

Feathered mummy mask, Tiahuanaco/Tiwanaku, Peru, South America.

life. The archeologist speculated that this mask and others discovered around the world were designed to deliberately hide a person's features. A mask would assure that evil spirits didn't recognize and waylay the departing soul.

In more recent times, survivors made life-size masks to record and preserve the features of loved ones and dead notables with materials like plaster of Paris, making it easy to form a reasonably accurate impression. Madame Tussaud, born Marie Gosoltz, started as an artisan specializing in death masks. She had made masks of people executed during the French Revolution—including the queen—many of which are still on display in her waxworks. Later, as a refugee in England, she began shaping wax models of heads instead of negative molds or plaster masks.

The development of photography eventually made the death mask more or less obsolete since a photo was relatively fast and easy. There was no mess involved, and the likeness was more lifelike.

See also: *Appeasing the dead, Effigies, Mementos.*

DECOMPOSITION (OR *DECAY*)

The instant a living thing expires, its cells begin to dissolve from the inside out. Deprived of oxygen, cell walls weaken, fluids escape, and remains start to decay and grow soft, crumble, or liquefy. Within days, leaked fluid causes the skin to blister and sag. Bacteria inside the corpse devour the dying cells and emit waste in the form of smelly gases that attract scavengers. Flesh-eating flies show up first, lay eggs, and soon their larvae or maggots speed to work. Carrion beetles arrive to partake of both flies and maggots. Eventually so much flesh has been nibbled or gnawed away and so much liquid released that the corpse collapses. Beetles with specialized mouthparts arrive to dine on tough ligaments and extant skin. Next come moths and bacteria that favor fur and feathers. When these various scavengers have done their work, all that's left is the skeleton.

Bones, like other parts of the body, have live cells, but bone matter consists mainly of calcium and other minerals, so unless predators work on the bones, it may take time and the elements a while to complete the job. It can take years for a skeleton to break down.

So in due course, everything that dies is dissolved by enzymes, liquefied by bacteria, digested by fungi, ingested by insects and predators, or otherwise put to new use.

Under certain conditions, decomposition doesn't play out in the usual way.

Fossilization happens when the remains of living things are sealed or preserved for millions of years in stone and amber or plant resin, and sometimes a body is preserved by freezing. The fully dressed five-thousand-year-old corpse of a man scientists call Otzi was discovered high in the Alps, where he'd been encased in ice. Researchers have also found and mapped the genetic code in the bone tissue of a frozen wooly mammoth in Siberia.

In very high, mountainous places or dry deserts, corpses can dehydrate, or mummify, and they're sometimes found in soggy peat bogs where cold temperatures and natural acids retard decay and where bacteria can't survive for lack of oxygen. Their bones are often eaten away by acidic water, but the skin and inner organs can be uncannily preserved, right down to a stomach bearing undigested evidence of a person's last meal. Archeologists think these "bog people," with their dark, leathery, "tanned" skin, were killed and ceremonially offered to the bogs between 2,000 and 3,600 years ago. Tollund Man, who died around 2,400 years ago, was so perfectly preserved that the people who discovered him in 1950 enlisted the police, thinking they'd happened on a recent murder victim.

See also: *Corpse, Embalming, Forensic science, Mummy.*

EFFIGIES

The custom of honoring or memorializing the dead with figures or effigies has a long history. Primitive people made little effigies of straw, cloth, or wood to represent themselves, fitting them to the corpse before burial so the dead spirit would not pine for those left behind or search them out.

In Tahiti, the priest who performed funeral rites might lay strips of plaintain leafstalk on the breast and under the arms of the corpse and say something along the lines of, "There are your family . . . there is your child . . . there is your wife . . . there is your father . . . and there is your mother. Be satisfied and look not for those who are left in this world."

When a twin died in Yoruba, West Africa, the mother might carry around both her surviving child and a small wooden figure roughly carved to resemble the dead twin in form and gender. The figure not only gave comfort to the living child, but theoretically gave the spirit of the deceased a place to retreat to without disturbing anyone.

During the ninth and tenth Egyptian dynasties, citizens who had been surrounded by servants in life were entombed with trays of miniature models showing vassals paying taxes in the form of animals or grain, bakers with baskets of bread on their heads, servants laboring. These effigies ensured that the deceased would be well cared for in the next realm, just as they had been on earth.

Effigies of important people in England and elsewhere were often crafted of beeswax, which was easy to sculpt and held its shape for years. Beeswax effigies served as temporary monuments in churches and cathedrals while the stonecutter worked on more permanent fare.

Westminster Abbey in London houses a collection of life-size, richly garbed effigies of such royal and notable figures as Queen Elizabeth I and King Charles II. Most are crafted of wax or wood, though the effigies of Richard II and Anne of Bohemia—who were originally depicted holding hands, though the

Ushebtis, servants for the deceased in the hereafter. Blue faience. Egypt, late period (713–332 BC). Louvre, Paris, France.

hands have since broken off—are made of gilded bronze, stamped all over with patterns and badges or crests.

See also: *Death masks.*

EMBALMING

The practice of preserving a body against decay has been around for thousands of years. Today in North America, the goal is keep the corpse intact for just a few days until funeral arrangements can be made, but the preserved mummies of ancient Egyptians and Incans have taught us much about the way people in these and other societies approached death—and life.

In the United States, demand for embalming spiked during the Civil War, when wealthy families no longer accepted the idea of collective burial on the battlefield. Embalmed soldiers could be transported home and honored with a proper burial.

Bodies can be preserved—on purpose or accidentally—with help from chemicals, freezing, fire, or smoke. Frozen soon after death, left in dry, hot sand, or otherwise allowed to dry out quickly, the body's soft tissue can't break down because bacteria and fungi can't grow in it, which is the case with accidental mummies, like the "bog people" discovered in acidic peat bogs in northern Europe over the years or in caves that contain gases that kill bacteria. A body sealed in an airtight coffin may also be preserved in this way.

In 2007 a well-preserved baby mammoth with trunk, eyes, and fur intact was found frozen in the permafrost of northwestern Siberia. While scientists have not yet found the kind of DNA that would make it feasible to clone the extinct animal, they are hopeful.

See also: *Cryonics, Decomposition, Mummy.*

EPITAPH

At one time an inscription placed on a tomb (*epi* means "to place something on"; *taphos* means "tomb"), the word "epitaph" now stands for pretty near any grave-marker message.

When and where a person lived had a lot to do with the tone of the tribute. While "Erected in memory of . . ." and "Here lies buried . . ." state the simple fact and keep a person's memory alive, other messages are more specific and reflective, recommending the deceased to God, urging survivors to be mindful of their own mortality ("Reader beware as you pass by / As you are now so once was I / As I am now so you will be / Prepare for death and follow me"), or expressing the feelings of the bereaved ("Sacred to the memory of . . . ," "Here lies cut down, like unripe fruit . . . ," "How could you, death / At once destroy / The husband's hope / The children's joy?" and "Farewell Bright soul a short farewell / Till we shall meet again Above . . .").

Some epitaphs are witty and poignant, expressing the personality now departed ("This life's a dream / And all things show it. / I thought so once and / Now I know it") or hinting at the way a person

THE BODY

of

BENJAMIN FRANKLIN

PRINTER

(LIKE THE COVER OF AN OLD BOOK ITS CONTENTS TORN OUT AND STRIPT OF ITS LETTERING AND GILDING),

LIES HERE, FOOD FOR WORMS.

BUT THE WORK SHALL NOT BE LOST

FOR IT WILL (AS HE BELIEVED) APPEAR ONCE MORE

in a

NEW AND MORE ELEGANT EDITION

REVISED AND CORRECTED

BY THE AUTHOR.

Epitaph composed by the young printer Benjamin Franklin. It never made it onto the statesman's gravestone, on which only these parting words appear: "Benjamin and Deborah Franklin, 1790."

throughout history by the search for a mythical fountain of youth.

The impulse was first recorded way back in ancient Mesopotamia or Sumer (modern Iraq), in the world's oldest literary masterpiece, *The Epic of Gilgamesh*. Afraid of death after his best friend succumbs, Gilgamesh lights out in search of eternal youth only to be informed by the goddess Shiduir, who runs an alehouse at the edge of the world:

> The life that you seek you will
>   never find:
> When the gods created mankind,
> Death they dispensed to mankind,
> Life they kept for themselves.

lived or died ("School is out, teacher has gone home" or "Here lies one whose life threads were cut asunder. She was struck dead by a clap of thunder"). Others pose violent threats ("I, Idameneus, built this tomb to my own glory. May Zeus utterly destroy anyone who disturbs it").

Just as tomb and gravestone art have evolved to reflect changes in society and spiritual orientation, so too have our parting words for our dead.
See also: *Consciousness, Gravestone, Tomb.*

Gilgamesh does eventually locate a plant that will make an old man young again, but while he's bathing in a pool, a snake steals it from him and devours the precious plant; this is why snakes shed their skins and grow young again in Mesopotamian myth, while humans grow old and die.

In Greek mythology, the gods have ambrosia and nectar, the food and drink of immortality, but humans have never ceased seeking their own insurance against death.

In the Middle Ages, alchemists set out to divine the secret properties of gold. Alchemy being part science, part mystical art, alchemists swore by a substance called the philosopher's stone, which they believed had the power to turn base metals into gold and to restore lost youth and vitality. Medieval alchemists reput-

ETERNAL LIFE (QUEST FOR)

If we can't live forever, and we're trying harder than ever, we can at least strive for a long, healthy life and maybe put things on hold until technical and medical advancements make the impossible possible.

Driven by a yearning for eternal youth and health, we have been preoccupied

edly brewed potions with magical properties—elixirs that extended their lives, at least in legend, for hundreds of years.

Asia, too, had a long tradition of brewing life-lengthening elixirs. Ancient Hindu medicine had a branch called Kaya Kulp, or the science of rejuvenation, with an emphasis on potions. One recipe called for climbing asparagus, yam, gingko fruit, wild dill, wild fennel, and "secret" ingredients. The secret ingredients aren't secret for nothing, though, and a parallel recipe features a single plant created by the gods to delay decay and death, an ingredient visible only to the most virtuous believers.

In the ancient Chinese religious tradition of Taoism, virtuous living leads to union with the Tao, a blessed state that features eternal life among its many other benefits. Taoist lore is replete with *Xians,* humans who practiced yoga and alchemy to achieve immortality, a reward for people sworn to solitude and ascetic virtue. Xians took on so much vital force in life that they carried on even after their bodies died. These happy immortals roamed the universe at will, convening from time to time at mythical peach banquets where they dined together on the bone marrow of the phoenix bird. Taoist alchemists used cinnabar in their concoctions, a mercury ore that also happens to be fatal. Historians surmise that during the Tang Dynasty, AD 618 to 907, up to seven rulers who partook of such elixirs died.

People in China's Bama County, northwest of Nanning, the capital of Guanxi, claim that singing folksongs and drinking a tonic of herbs and gutted poisonous snakes steeped for months in rice wine help account for the record-making longevity of its population. A 1994 survey found that of the county's 230,000 inhabitants, 81 had exceeded the age of one hundred. People aged ninety to ninety-nine numbered 226. On November 1, 1991, at the Japanese Tokyo World Natural Science Convention, Bama ranked fifth in longevity in the world.

In his 1933 novel, *Lost Horizon,* James Hilton describes the hidden Himalayan valley of Shangri-la, where people enjoy vigor and smooth-skinned beauty for centuries. A real if remote valley called Hunza in the mountains of northern Pakistan evidently shares many of the imaginary Shangri-la's traits—not least a healthy, long-lived population—and has been called its real-life counterpart. But the name for Hilton's fictional paradise now equates with any remote or unattainable state of bliss.

Name the era, and there was at least one method or "medical" treatment touted for postponing old age—from cold water cures to "tonics" with names like Burdock Blood Bitters. For a while, getting yourself injected with the blood of a youthful donor was all the rage. In the fifteenth century, Pope Innocent VIII is said to have tried to extend his life with transfusions of the blood of young boys.

Today, technical advances from cloning to Botox and chemical peels seem to promise their own superficial versions of Shangri-la.

See also: *Cryonics.*

EULOGY

A speech that honors a dead person.
See also:: *Memorial service.*

EUPHEMISMS

There are at least two hundred ways of saying that someone has died without saying it, from old standards like "passed away" or "passed on" to livelier fare such as "kicked the bucket," "bit the dust," "bought the farm," or "gave up the ghost." The "deceased" can sleep "in Abraham's bosom," "with the Tribbles"—a *Star Trek* favorite—or like Luka Brazzi in *The Godfather,* "with fishes." You can "cash in your chips" or shuffle off your "mortal coil," and once you do, morticians will refer to you as "the loved one" or the "dearly departed" and to themselves as "grief therapists" entrusted with an "undertaking" (burial). After that, you're "pushing up" daisies or parsley.
See also: *Consciousness of death.*

EUTHANASIA

The word literally means "a good death," and euthanasia is the act of ending a life painlessly, to relieve the incurable suffering of terminal or long-term illness.

Passive euthanasia means withdrawing whatever treatment is sustaining a person's life. Patients who are mentally competent have the right to refuse medical treatment, triggering their deaths. But what if they ask friends or relatives to aid their efforts by providing drugs? What if a doctor intervenes at the patient's request? This euthanasia is assisted suicide, and in most countries, it's illegal. Doctors who carry out such "mercy killings" can be prosecuted for murder.

"Dr. Death" to his foes, Michigan M.D. Jack Kevorkian has helped several terminally ill patients end their lives and has been acquitted four times on murder charges. In 1999 he was found guilty and was sentenced ten to fifteen years for second-degree murder.

Worldwide, voluntary euthanasia became legal for the first time on July 1, 1996, in Australia's Northern Territory. Four terminally ill patients died assisted by their doctors before the law, which lacked national support, was overturned by the Australian Parliament the following March.

Although the state of Oregon passed a "death with dignity" act in 1994 and permits assisted suicide, the medical establishment remains largely opposed to the practice. According to the assisted suicide website of the Euthanasia Research and Guidance Organization (ERGO), the only four places in the world today that *"openly* and *legally* . . . authorize active assistance" are Oregon, Switzerland, Belgium, and the Netherlands. "Two doctors must be involved in Oregon, Belgium, and the Netherlands, plus a psychologist if there are doubts about the patient's competency," the website notes.

A 2005 survey of one thousand doctors found that 57 percent believed it is ethical to assist a patient seeking to end his or her own life. But for some, such aid conflicts with the Hippocratic oath, a basis of modern medicals ethics, which reads: "I swear . . . that I will prescribe treatment to the best of my ability and judgment for the good of the sick, and never for a harmful or illicit purpose. I will give no poisonous drug, even if asked to, nor make any such suggestion."

In the United States, the controversy exploded in 2005 when the impending death of Terry Schiavo, a paralyzed Florida woman, hit the news. If anything worthwhile came of the bitter struggle between her parents and husband over her fate—which echoed out into the nation at large—it was increased public awareness of the value of living wills and method-of-disposition documents. Many have been inspired to make decisions about their life and death in advance, before they become too ill or impaired to choose.
See also: *Suicide.*

EVIL EYE

One of the first things solemn spectators in Hollywood movies and TV dramas do when a body has expired is close its eyes. Why? Maybe we close the eyes of the dead for the same reason we don't speak ill of them: to avoid drawing attention to ourselves. There are many traditional interpretations of the evil eye, most relating to envy, but many feel sure that once a corpse fixes its gaze on you, you aren't long for this world. If the eyes remain open, they're searching out the next one to die. The near universal tradition of closing the eyes was already in place back when the early Hebrew scrip-

tures were written, and to keep the lids closed long enough for rigor mortis to set in, small weights were sometimes used. Coins served this purpose well—and jibed with the ancient idea that the living should furnish the dead with a toll for crossing into the next world.
See also: *Appeasing the dead, Hades.*

EXHUMATION

A body might be exhumed or disinterred—dug up and removed from its grave—for any number of reasons, as when the deceased died under suspicious circumstances and law enforcement officials suspect foul play or when the body had been wrongly identified at the outset.

Bodies may also be removed from overcrowded cemeteries or desirable plots of land to be cremated or relocated to alternative gravesites, ossuaries, or catacombs. In a land-scarce country like Singapore, for instance, graves are regularly exhumed to make room for new bodies, development, and construction. A Feng Shui website lays out the appropriate rites and rituals in the event that exhumation becomes necessary. These include consulting the Chinese horoscopes of the deceased and family to select an auspicious date for the removal, lifting the bones in a prescribed order, and washing some of them in a basin of rice wine. The bones should be carried away in a white bag with an identification tag under a Chinese wood and canvas umbrella to "guide the soul of the dead" out of the grave for cremation. Not surprisingly, conflict can occur—for example, between U.S. construction companies and some Native American groups—when local authorities allow land that contains burial sites to be put to other uses.

Sometimes loved ones have a body exhumed so they can re-inter it in a location that feels more appropriate religiously or personally, as when Sophia and Una Hawthorne, the wife and daughter of nineteenth-century American author Nathaniel Hawthorne, were exhumed from their graves in England in 2006. The Hawthornes were symbolically reunited in Concord, Massachusetts, in June, with a horse-drawn carriage—the same one believed to have carried Hawthorne's casket to Sleepy Hollow Cemetery in 1861—transporting the remains to the family plot. A crowd of some two hundred people gathered under a tent on the lawn of the Old Manse, the Hawthorne family's first home, for a service after the private interment.

Bodies may also be unearthed to help solve significant historical mysteries or to allow archeologists to learn about past cultures from human remains. The Egyptian pharaoh Tutankhamen, commonly known as King Tut, was exhumed in 2005 to determine his cause of death, which is still under investigation. In 2007 archeologists removed the remains of a Viking queen and a younger woman from a grassy burial mound in Oseberg, Norway. Was the second woman a young servant—sacrificed to be the queen's companion in the afterlife? Or were the two mother and daughter, dead of the same disease and buried together in AD 834?

Scientists hope a DNA test of the two bodies will yield an answer.

See also: *Burial, Burial—double, Forensic science, Funerary rites.*

EXTINCTION

When the last member of a species dies, that species is gone forever, extinct. Scientists believe almost a third of the world's species face extinction before the year 2100, and that between one and one hundred species are being lost around the world every *day*, mostly on account of habitat destruction.

Cloning or "reviving" an extinct species—an ambition illustrated in the book and film *Jurassic Park*—would require undamaged DNA from that animal. Dinosaur remains are almost always fossilized, so the odds of discovering usable DNA aren't good, and while scientists have mapped the genetic code of the extinct wooly mammoth, the DNA they've procured is too damaged to undergo cloning.

FLORA

Pollen traces found with a skull in the soil in Shanidar Cave in Iraq have led some researchers to speculate that Neanderthals may have used flowers to mark burial sites or adorn the bodies of their dead.

A discovery at a Bronze Age burial mound on the Black Mountain in Carmarthenshire, Wales, hints that floral tributes on graves date back at least four thousand years. Analysis of microscopic pollen grains found in the soil surrounding the grave of a child there suggests the burial was accompanied by a tribute of meadowsweet, a flower with creamy white clusters.

Though plant remains are occasionally found inside coffins, there is scant evidence of flowers being used ceremonially at funerals until the sixteenth century. By the late 1500s, mourners regularly carried sprigs of yew, cypress, or other evergreens. Aromatic rosemary, which flowers in winter, was a popular choice, and coffins sometimes had bunches tied to their sides.

White lilies, linked by Christians to the Madonna and purity, are often placed on graves, as are palm leaves, the symbol of Palm Sunday and eternal life.

During Mexico's Day of the Dead, trails of yellow marigold petals—the *cempauchil* or "flower of the dead"—lead souls home to the offerings prepared in their honor.

As J. K. Rowling illustrated in the *Harry Potter* books, the mandrake is a plant with personality. When you pull it from the ground—which must be done at midnight, according to folklore—the breaking fibers sound a "shriek." In folklore, the plant flourished in graveyards, attaching itself to the spirits of the dead, so in Germany people fashioned mandrakes into dolls, dressing them with care and nestling them with the corpse in the casket.

The poppy, which stands for sleep and dreams, has also become a vivid symbol of lives lost in the two World Wars, thanks in part to Canadian poet John McCrae's famous lines: "In Flander fields where poppies blow / Between the crosses row on row . . ."

Today the phrase "in lieu of flowers" often appears in obituaries, a trend that may diminish the importance of this ancient form of tribute.

See also: *Symbols.*

FOOD–FOR THE DEAD

Many cultures provide food for the spirits of the dead. The ancient Greeks buried their dead with a costly jar of honey, with the rich and powerful rating many jars. In rural Mexico, Christians still place cooked fruit on church altars so departed loved ones may feast, and during the Day of the Dead offer spirits the food and drink they favored in life—everything from breads and biscuits, sugar figures, candied pumpkin, and fruit pastes to cooked chicken or turkey *mole,* a thick, spicy sauce made with chili peppers and cacao. Toda tribesmen of southern India use buffalo milk as their staple food, so they may slaughter select dairy cattle when a herdsman dies, giving him a start toward building up a herd in the spirit world.

The demons and undead of folklore—from the *lilats* of ancient Babylonia and Assyria to the German *alp* to the *molong* of Malaysia—often feed on or drink from the living, so offerings of food and water might also satisfy potentially dangerous appetites. Poppy seeds were a common choice in medieval Europe, and the dead were said to ingest them at a rate of only one per year—no surprise, given the flower's trace narcotic proper-

FORBIDDEN FRUIT

When Hades kidnaps Demeter's beautiful daughter, Persephone, to rule at his side as queen of the Underworld, the girl mourns below even as her powerful mother mourns above. Demeter is goddess of the harvest, so all nature suffers with them: fields and flowers wither, trees shed their leaves; animals and people starve.

The other gods on Mount Olympus plead, but Demeter vows never again to bless the earth until her beloved Persephone is restored to her. So Zeus commands gloomy Hades to give up his young bride. But before the girl can flee to her mother's embrace, it's revealed that Persephone has tasted the food of the dead, nibbling thoughtlessly at a handful of pomegranate seeds from Hades' garden. Doomed to penance by this oversight, she must return to the Underworld for part of each year, languishing a month below for every seed ingested.

In her absence, winter blankets the earth. But when sunlight touches Persephone's hair and her joyful laughter reaches Demeter's ears, the meadows blaze green again.

Frederic Leighton (1830–1896), *The Return of Persephone,* c. 1891 (oil on canvas).

ties—a task that kept them sedated and out of mind.

See also: *Appeasing the dead, Undead.*

FOOD-FOR MOURNERS

Breaking bread together after a death is one way of affirming life and uniting in grief. The meal may be lavish or spare, but usually takes place, and some are more symbolic than others.

Some anthropologists have reported the practice of funerary cannibalism, eating human remains to draw in the vitality of the deceased, to spiritually reabsorb their life into the family or clan, or to disable an enemy. The Amazonian Yanomami, for instance, traditionally cremate and ingest human ashes with banana paste.

A traditional rite among some Balinese involves laying a body on a table with water slowly dripping over it and flowing, together with any natural drainage, into a cradle of unhusked rice, essentially coating the rice in corpse water. Once the body is interred, the rice is shaken from its husks, cooked as usual, and formed to suggest a tiny human before being served to the rest of the tribe.

In Ecuador, a mourner may clip a lock of hair from the body and burn it, mixing the ashes with some of the food served at the funeral feast, and guests are expected to partake.

In medieval England, funeral rites ended with a communal meal, where gentlemen and priests enjoyed lamb, veal, and roast mutton with stewed prunes, and the wealthy left a dole for the poor in the form of spiced bread and wine or bread and cheese. Mourners might also provide meal money for fellow members of their trade or guild. The shopping list for one medieval funeral feast circa 1309 called for five pigs, one hare, five sheep, thirteen hens, nineteen geese, 1 1/2 gallons of oysters, nine capons, 1 1/2 carcasses of beef, wine, ale, eggs, bread, and fifty pounds of wax for candles. The poor got a roll and a liquor concoction of "dog's nose" made with rum and ale.

At the funeral of Samuel Pepys' brother Tom in 1664, mourners enjoyed "six biscuits a-piece, and what they pleased of burnt claret," and a noblewoman's burial meal of around the same time consisted of "various wines, cakes, biscuits, dried fruit, pippins, plums, quinces, gooseberries, almonds, and macaroons." People in this era often gathered in the same room as the coffin with guests sitting, standing, and imbibing around it.

Before the Reformation in England, food was often given to mourners to purchase their prayers for the deceased's soul. But many Puritans viewed feasting after a funeral as inappropriate to the solemnity of the occasion, so post-Reformation funeral meals were merely for "remembrance."

In Belgium, funeral food includes slices of crisp black bread called *simnel* cake, or "soul bread," and chocolate cake.

Whatever the symbolism or recipe,

bringing food to grieving families continues to be an important way for friends to lend support and help. When a member of a Muslim family has died, mourners may not cook for themselves for forty days. When the formal grieving period is over, a family may invite supportive relatives and friends over for a meal, preparing the dead person's seven favorite foods and serving a little to each guest.

FORENSIC SCIENCE

In China way back in 1248, a book called *Hsi Duan Yu* (The Washing Away of Wrongs) described methods for distinguishing a natural death from an unnatural one. For example, damaged cartilage on the neck and pressure marks on the throat suggest death by strangulation.

Forensic science has come a long way, but observation and analysis are still key. After a crime occurs, law enforcement teams comb the scene. They assess all physical evidence, some obvious and telltale, such as bullets, fingerprints, and bloodstains, and some, like carpet threads and hair traces, more subtle (if no less suspect). They also compare details about grease, paint, glass, and so forth with evidence found in a suspect's possession—data that's as likely to be used in the courtroom as in the lab.

Any number of specialists may be brought in to contribute their particular know-how to a case, from the forensic pathologist who conducts the autopsy to a toxicologist, who can detect drugs or

DOWN ON THE FARM

Researchers at the University of Tennessee Forensic Anthropology Facility, popularly known as "the Body Farm," study postmortem change in an outdoor field laboratory started by Dr. William M. Bass in 1972. Donated human remains are squashed into car trunks, spread over with branches, submerged in water, left in direct sunlight, or otherwise dispersed on three acres near the University Medical Center.

Roughly forty bodies, surrounded by razor wire and wooden fences, rot outdoors at any given time as researchers observe variable rates of decay and study factors like which insects attend the body and when.

The Body Farm gives law enforcement officials and students who are training in forensic anthropology and skeletal biology an invaluable hands-on education in the science of human decomposition.

poisons in the body, to the odontologist who examines the victim's teeth, comparing them with dental records for identification. Forensic botanists study any plant matter, seeds, or pollens that might have been found on a body at a crime scene, while forensic entomologists work out the time of death by studying insects collected on or around the corpse.

Dactylography is the study of fingerprints as a method of identification. Scientist Alec Jeffreys, who spearheaded the development of DNA fingerprinting, used the technique to identify a skeleton found in Brazil in 1979. Comparing the bones to those of living relatives, Jeffreys confirmed that the remains had once been Josef Mengele, the notorious Nazi war criminal from Auschwitz who escaped after World War II to South America, eluding the authorities for decades. Finding his remains was an act of symbolic closure for many Holocaust victims and their families.

DNA research and testing have dramatically changed the way scientists solve crimes. DNA, or deoxyribonucleic acid, can be found in almost every living cell in every living organism, and holds the genetic information of a cell. It can be extracted from blood, semen—even the saliva left on the back of a postage stamp.

In the United States, the FBI introduced a DNA database in 1998, and by 2001, many states were beginning to create DNA databases with genetic profiles of convicted felons.

FOX SISTERS, THE

As of March 31, 1848, the walls of the Fox farmhouse in Hydesville, New York, had been echoing for more than a week with inexplicable rapping and bumping noises, keeping the family inside awake and on edge. That night, alarmed by their daughters' cries, John and Margaret Fox rushed upstairs to find Maggie, age thirteen, and Kate, age eleven, talking back while the walls resounded.

Kate leaped out of bed and began snapping her fingers as she circled the room, commanding, "Follow me," and the unseen presence—Kate dubbed him "Mr. Splitfoot"—obeyed, the raps trailing along behind her.

Neighbors were summoned to play witness. Through a tedious method of rap-and-response—at first, two raps for yes, silence for no, and later, raps corresponding to letters of the alphabet—the presence revealed itself to be the spirit of a murdered peddler, long buried under the house. In the coming days, men entered the cellar with picks and shovels, excavating until rising groundwater deterred them. Strangers, meanwhile, arrived on foot, by horse and buggy, and in rented carriages. Families staked tents in surrounding fields, lit bonfires, milled outside the farmhouse, and peered in Fox family windows. At night, curiosity seekers trickled in to test the resident "spirit." Chairs were lined up, and Maggie, Kate, and Mrs. Fox oversaw the visitations and fielded questions.

By May, so many pilgrims had descended on the house that Maggie and Kate were sent to stay with relatives in and around Rochester. Not surprisingly, wherever the girls went, the raps went too. The pace of communication picked up when Kate and her teenage niece, Lizzie, proved able to enter a trance state and confer with those "on the other side." Parlor séances became the rage, and invitations for "tea and table-tilting" proliferated.

The following November, Maggie Fox

and her eldest sister—Lizzie's mother, Leah—demonstrated their unusual gifts at Corinthian Hall, Rochester's largest public auditorium. People lined up at dawn to see them, and by nine o'clock there were some seven hundred on hand, with tickets being scalped as at a concert or baseball game today. The sisters endured three rounds of exacting tests, evoking their noisy specter time and again and betraying no evidence of trickery.

This was a time when faith and ideas about the afterlife, for many, had been undermined by science. A family of otherwise ordinary farm girls had somehow tapped into society's increasing hunger for proof of the continuity of life, and a new religious movement was born, making them international celebrities in the process.

Forty years after those first eerie rap-pings, Maggie Fox decried spiritualism in front of a packed assembly at New York's Academy of Music. It was all a hoax, she said. She and her sisters had made the raps by manipulating their toe joints. Not long after, however, she shocked her followers anew by reversing her position, reclaiming her faith in a spirit realm.

Were the Fox sisters charlatans swept up in the excitement of a childhood prank? Or had they really raised the "veil" separating this world from that? Were they conduits or clever players? Either way they—or what they repre-sented—intrigued many prominent and sensible people, and their legacy persists in celebrity mediums, like Sylvia Brown, who cater to millions.

The *Boston Journal* reported on Novem-ber 23, 1904, that a decaying portion of the old cellar wall of the famous

Hydesville "spook house" had revealed "an almost entire human skeleton between the earth and crumbling walls, undoubtedly that of the wandering peddler, who is claimed to have been murdered in east room of the house and body hidden in cellar."

The Fox cottage was dismantled in April 1916 and transferred to the Lily Dale Spiritual Association of Lily Dale, New York. It burned down in 1955, but the tin peddler's pack—together with the Fox family Bible—is still exhibited in the museum there.

See also: *Houdini, Lily Dale, Medium, Spiritualism.*

FUNERARY RITES

How we part ways depends on our beliefs. The Hopi in Arizona bury a body with next to no ceremony and no formal gathering, but most cultures enact rituals for their dead.

Such rites may begin even before death. A dying Catholic, for instance, receives last rites from a priest. A dying Muslim may wish to face the direction of Mecca, the holy city where the prophet Muhammad was born.

Funerary rites aid the spirit in its passage to the other world or ensure a safe return from it, as in the cycle of perpetual rebirth described in the Tibetan Book of the Dead. Lest the deceased be waylaid by evil spirits or wind up an angry ghost, we keep careful watch over the body. In some traditions, a body must be washed a certain number of times or covered in colored cloth. As Katherine Ashenburg notes in her book, *The Mourner's Dance: What We Do When People Die,* "The Jew in ancient times begged pardon of the body before washing it (one of many apologies addressed to the dead body in cultures all around the world) and buried some of his favorite possessions with him (another widespread custom) at least partly to placate spirit." We light candles, incense, or lanterns to guide the dead. We open windows to set them free. During the funeral procession, their feet must point in a particular direction, usually feet first, as human beings tend to come into life headfirst and must leave the other way. And when a procession exits the house, we leave the door open until the funeral party comes back or pour water over the threshold to discourage the spirit from likewise returning.

We seem to have mixed motives where our dead are concerned. Some rites honor or appease the newly departed, while others comfort or safeguard those left behind, the "survivors." These goals overlap but are often, at heart, precautionary.

Often family and friends gather together to view the body, which helps people accept the death. Until the mid-twentieth century, ancient Irish superstitions prevailed in many Newfoundland fishing villages. A dead man's bed might be turned down on the first night of a wake, his pipe and slippers placed nearby, while after the funeral, all the chairs were overturned to confuse and discourage his spirit from returning.

In pre-Communist China, the simple act of closing a coffin lid could prove perilous. Bystanders took several steps backward or even left the room lest their shadows be enclosed with the corpse in the coffin, ill affecting their health.

Often a priest or other religious figure performs special rites at the funeral service and family members praise the dead. Mourners may remain still and solemn or wail and chant, as suits their culture. There may be a procession to the burial place.

Beginning in the 1800s in some southern cities in the United States, most notably New Orleans, funeral processions featured a brass band. On the way to the churchyard, they played a slow, mournful hymn or dirge but on the way back struck up spirited renditions of tunes like "When the Saints Go Marching In" or "Oh, Didn't He Ramble." On the return trip, mourners summoned passersby into the procession. Tourists scoured local papers for funeral parade listings, flocking there to observe or even participate. The hip-hop funeral is a contemporary offshoot; in 2003, rapper Soulja Slim's procession drew thousands to the streets. Since Hurricane Katrina, which devastated New Orleans in the summer of 2005, such spirited parades are rare.

Most funerals end with the burial or cremation of the body. In Ecuador and other countries, family members may dance all the way back from the cemetery and continue dancing till nightfall.

The Chinese burn bundles of paper "money" and other representations—pictures of food, clothing, jewelry, even modern conveniences like laptops—on the funeral pyre to provide loved ones with whatever they may need in the afterlife and ensure an auspicious journey, while in a more long-term gesture, a Muslim may read his holy book, the Koran, from beginning to end as a gift to the person who has died.

After the fact, we may visit the grave of the deceased with offerings of flowers, flags, or small stones—all gestures,

according to some anthropologists, symbolically intended to appease the dead, to keep them content, keep them "away."

"Perhaps leaving a small stone on a tomb originally represented a hope that the spirit would stay buried," notes Katherine Ashenburg in *The Mourner's Dance,* "but today it works as a poignant sign that someone remembers the person buried there, that someone still visits his last resting place."

Usually religion dictates funeral and burial rites, but the U.S. population is increasingly secular. A May 2007 Gallup Poll revealed that 86 percent of Americans believe in God, down from 90 percent in 2004. Baby boomers, the 76 million people born between 1946 and 1964, have fewer traditional or religious bonds than past generations and are increasingly confronting death in the form of aging parents and peers. This has prompted funeral directors to get creative. There are some twenty-two thousand funeral homes in the United States, which bury more than 2 million people each year to the tune of $13 billion.

Americans hire career and retirement coaches, personal trainers, wedding planners, and pet whisperers, so it's no surprise that today's funeral directors are being called upon to act as party or event planners, staging casino funerals in Las Vegas and the sorts of butterfly and dove releases popular at weddings. Whether it's a memorial service on a golf green, a procession of Harleys, or a well-produced "tribute video" of the proceedings, the consumer demand for end-of-life services that reflect the personality of the departed is being heard.

In Germany there were almost 150,000 more deaths than births in 2006, a continuation of a trend that has seen a large portion of the country's population age dramatically in recent years. In 2007 a new TV channel, EosTV, began catering to that demographic by providing exclusive twenty-four-hour-a-day documentary coverage of themes like aging, death, and dying.

See also: *Appeasing the dead, Bon, Burial, Cremation, Day(s) of the Dead, Mourning, Wake.*

GENOCIDE

Genocide is the large-scale systematic and state-sponsored or condoned killing of a group of people on the basis of race, ethnicity, or religion. Victims of genocide are often buried heaped together in mass graves or landfill pits, a tactic that objectifies and dehumanizes the corpses and symbolically serves the literal goal of blotting out a portion of the population.

It's an ancient practice, but the word itself was first coined to describe the Nazi occupation of Poland as an act meant to do away with Polish identity. It was in response to the Nazis' genocide of the Jews and of ethnic groups such as the Gypsies that the Convention on the Prevention and Punishment of the Crime of Genocide was adopted by the United Nations in 1948. The idea behind the convention was that genocide is an international concern—not simply a matter of domestic jurisdiction—and those responsible must be held individually accountable. However, genocide has sometimes been challenging to legally establish, as evidence can

be hard to gather and controversy may arise over what nation, court, or tribunal should try the case.

In addition to the Holocaust, other twentieth-century genocides include the slaughter of some 1.5 million Christian Armenians in 1915 by the then Ottoman state, eager to redefine itself as ethnically Turkish. In the late 1970s, the Khmer Rouge, a militant Communist regime led by Pol Pot, sought to redefine the country of Cambodia as a peasant collective. Anyone not fitting the party profile—be they ethnic Vietnamese, Buddhist, Muslim Cham, intellectual, or homosexual—was at risk, and more than 1.5 million people were slain in ghastly "killing fields."

In the 1990s, the breakup of the former federated republic of Yugoslavia led to a series of Balkan wars and two genocidal assaults, one on the Bosnian Muslims by Christian Serbs, the other on the Albanians of Kosovo. These, together with the genocide of the Tutsis in Rwanda in 1994, resulted in the development of the United Nations' International Criminal

Tribunal for the Former Yugoslavia and the Tribunal for Rwanda and in the 1998 formation of the International Criminal Court for Genocide and Major Human Rights Violations.

While as of this writing the United Nations has stopped short of calling the conflict in Sudan's arid and impoverished Darfur "genocide," two hundred thousand people have died there and some 2 million are currently suffering in refugee camps with severe shortages of food, water, and medicine after fleeing four-plus years of rebel fighting. Sudan's government and progovernment Arab militias are accused of war crimes against the region's black African population. Peacekeeping forces and aid agencies are actively seeking a solution. See also: *Murder, War.*

GHOSTS

"All argument is against it, but all belief is for it," Samuel Johnson said of the idea that spirits venture back from the other side. Though ghosts have never been scientifically documented, a 2005 Gallup Poll revealed that 32 percent of Americans believe in them.

A ghost is the spirit of a dead person— as distinct from an apparition, a broader term including manifestations like dead horses and phantom schooners. Ghosts may be glimpsed just once, appear repeatedly on significant dates, or outright "haunt" a location.

A wraith or, in Germany, *doppelgänger* or "double-goer," is a person's spiritual

double that may be so lifelike witnesses mistake it for the real person. A wraith sighting usually serves as an omen that the person in question isn't long for this world, though sometimes a living person will meet his or her own *doppelgänger* and live to tell. The German poet Goethe is a famous case. Goethe reputedly encountered his phantom as he rode away from a visit. The figure wore an unfamiliar gray suit with gold lace, and when Goethe found himself on the same road en route to see the same person eight years later, it dawned on him that he was decked out in the very suit his double had worn.

"Crisis" apparitions are ghosts that appear to friends and relatives when a person dies at some distance or is involved in an accident, and while you won't get a look at poltergeists ("noisy spirits"), they're famous for hurling objects around the room, showering windows with stones, and toppling furniture.

Folklore about ghosts abounds in nearly every culture. A candle burning blue suggests the presence of a spirit in the house. If a mother dies in childbirth, she'll remain behind in spirit form to assure her child's safety. Unrequited lovers make frequent ghostly appearances. A Danish tradition holds that you can pin a ghost to the spot with a wooden post; pull the post up, however, and the ghost goes free.

In Japanese lore, spirits are angry and impure after death. Death rites performed over the course of many years cleanse the soul and deliver it from emotions like anger, envy, and jealousy. If not led aloft by the prayers and good will of the living, spirits drift between the shadow and living realms or linger on earth as ghosts. During the Heian era (794–1185), ghostly spirits were blamed for disease, plague, and famine. In the Kamakura era (1185–1333), they were thought to morph into raccoons, foxes, and other small animals and tempt people astray. Vengeful spirits were a popular theme in eighteenth-century Kabuki theater.

Since ancient times people have believed that a person's spirit can exist outside the body, that the spirit lives on in some way after death, and modern parapsychologists posit that spirits project their presence into the mind of the living using extrasensory perception (ESP). Clairvoyants and other "sensitives" are equipped to tune in to these messages, be they compassionate assurances that death is not the end or reflections of individual refusal to exit quietly.

Founded in London in 1882 in response to the spiritualist craze that swept England in the 1870s, the Society for Psychical Research (SPR) was the first major organization committed to the scientific study of paranormal activity, including ghost and poltergeist phenomena, ESP, hypnosis, and other topics. The creator of Sherlock Holmes, Sir Arthur Conan Doyle, an avowed spiritualist, was an SPR member, and eventually psychoanalyst Sigmund Freud and psychiatrist Carl Jung joined the society. By 1885 the American Society for Psychical Research (ASPR) was formed in Boston, later relocating to its current location in New York City. Psychologist and philosopher William James served as SPR president from 1894 to 1895; at various points in time, the same position was held by mathematicians, physicists, scholars, a prime minister, and the inventor of the radiometer.

Science today offers a number of explanations for ghosts and hauntings. One theory credits sound waves. Very low frequency standing waves are sometimes trapped in buildings, causing vibrations that not only make us feel edgy but outright jiggle our eyeballs and blur our vision, making us "see" ghosts. See also: *Haunting*.

GOTH

The original Goths were an eastern Germanic tribe that helped bring down the Roman Empire. For better or worse, their name came to mean "barbarian." During the Renaissance in Europe, people dubbed medieval architecture "gothic" to set it apart from the preferred classical style, but in England, the writer Horace Walpole fueled a "revival" of interest in gothic ruins.

Walpole, as it happens, also introduced the gothic novel form with his 1764 book *The Castle of Otranto*. As the genre gained popularity, the word "gothic" evoked morbidity and bleakness, and established the supernatural mood and symbols that would go on to influence horror lit and movies, from Bela Lugosi's *Dracula* to *The Hunger* to *The Crow*: ruined castles and churches, graveyards, brooding vampires and pining ghosts, scheming heirs and family curses, claustrophobia, camp, and melodrama.

Contemporary goth subculture draws from these and other elements. It began in the post-punk 1980s in the gothic rock and death rock music scene defined by bands like Bauhaus, Siouxsie and the Banshees, and the Damned. There's a shared aesthetic, but Goths hail from different backgrounds and have varying religious and political affiliations. Many are drawn because they don't conform to society at large, and the goth lifestyle is a way to know community. It doesn't hurt, too, to be fascinated with the otherworldly and mystical, to be cynical, tragically roman-

tic, campy, theatrical, and committed to tolerance, individuality, and creativity.

Goth fashion tends to be period inspired, drawing on medieval, Renaissance, and Victorian models as well as androgyny, death rock, and punk. Black is always the new black, be it clothing, eyeliner, dyed hair, or fingernails. Piercings and religious symbols like ankhs and crucifixes are common accessories.

Some adults perceive of goth as nihilistic, negative, and despairing, claiming the movement draws already marginalized teens and further alienates them from the mainstream. Critical concern peaked after the Columbine High School massacre, carried out by two students wrongly aligned with the subculture. High visibility may assure solidarity and belonging, but many Goths also endure prejudice with humor and a flair for self-parody.

See also: *Music.*

GRAVE GOODS

Archeologists have found grave goods in the tombs of our earliest civilizations. Mesopotamian kings were buried with furniture, musical instruments, and gambling gear to equip them for the next life. Egyptians interred their pharaohs with gold and jewels and model boats. A Chinese emperor was buried with an army of some eight thousand life-size terracotta warriors to guard him in the afterworld, while the burial caves of Aleut hunters were stocked with fine spears and harpoons.

By the sentimental nineteenth century, the "goods" might be less lavish or practical than personal—perhaps a handkerchief, a thimble, some small token or tribute. But when painter-poet Dante Gabriel Rossetti's wife Elizabeth died of tuberculosis, he buried her with the most intimate of mementos: a manuscript of his own poetry, which he nestled between her beloved cheek and her auburn hair. This, of course, in the days before photocopy machines.

Forever is a long time. Years passed and grief receded, with Rossetti plagued by second thoughts. He enlisted friends to furtively—at the risk of fines and imprisonment—dig up the body and recall his precious verses. He had each sheet carefully dried and went on to secure swift literary success for them.

Grave goods may also include objects of symbolic import to the deceased.

Film star Bela Lugosi, for instance, was buried in the cape that he wore in his Count Dracula role.

GRAVESTONE

A gravestone, headstone, or tombstone is a permanent marker situated over or near a burial site, often but not always made of stone or slate: materials like iron, wood, marble, or bronze might also be used, depending on regional availability and the prevailing fashion.

In colonial America until the 1660s, only a small percentage of people—less than half—had grave markers at all. Mounds of earth, piled stones, or wooden posts might serve, and while some graves had permanent markers in the form of roughly inscribed fieldstones, there were very few carved stone markers until after the mid-seventeenth century. "It just wasn't a custom," says Laurel K. Gabel of the Association for Gravestone Studies. "For the early colonists, the soul was what mattered. The body was just a shell."

Artistically the first stones were very small, spare, and simple, carved with capital letters. Skulls, crossed bones, coffins, and other death emblems or symbols appeared first, and then, gradually, generic faces (cherubs were depicted only later). While no effort was made to represent the deceased or craft a portrait of any individual, these figures reflected each carver's individual style.

HADES

Charon, an old boatman in Greek mythology, ferried the souls of dead people across the River Styx or the Acheron River to the ancient Greek underworld. Guarded by a fearsome three-headed dog named Cerberus, Hades was a dreary, sunless land where bored shades languished and forgot and pined forevermore. Homer said you were better off being a beggar in the land of the living than a king in that place of the shadows. Only great heroes and patriots—who celebrated their victories as immortals in an alter-afterlife in Elysium—could escape Hades. Those who'd earned the wrath of the gods were dispatched to the dismal pit of Tartarus, a region reserved for punishment.

See also: *Afterlife, Food—for the dead.*

HALLOWEEN

The word comes from the Middle English *hallowen* for "hallowed" or "sacred" and the shortening of *evening* to *e'en*.

Many of the holidays we celebrate today have their origins in pagan religious practices. Pagans believed not in a single all-powerful God but in numerous gods, goddesses, and deities bound to the natural world and its cycles.

Halloween stems from the Roman Catholic feasts of All Saints' Day and All Souls' Day, known together as Hallowtide, which drew on earlier pagan traditions.

The ancient Romans believed that during the festival of Lemuria, in May, the dead left their graves to be with the living. In the seventh century, Pope Boniface IV replaced the old Lemuria with All Saints' Day, a May 13 observance honoring the Catholic saints. In AD 834, Pope Gregory IV shifted All Saints' Day to November 1 to muscle out Samhain—a word that means "summer's end" in the Gaelic languages—an ancient festival of the dead the Celts celebrated before they were converted to Christianity. The Church further designated November 2 All Souls' Day, a time to honor the stationary dead at their graves.

But these clever efforts never quite eclipsed local custom. October 31, the night that came to be called All Saints' Eve, was the last of the Celtic year, marking the end of autumn harvest and the coming of winter. The Celts believed the barrier between the worlds of the living and dead weakened on that night, that souls of the dead and other supernatural figures slipped through to rub elbows with mortals. They must be rewarded for their trouble, or appeased, so people made food offerings and essentially threw a party, distracting the interlopers with feasting and mischief until the rooster crowed and they wandered back from whence they came, and the new year began.

Legends about the dead being abroad that night, some more malevolent than others, have hung on. Later Europeans believed that Satan, witches, and demons also had free access on All Saints' Eve, and in one story these malefactors gather and dance till dawn on top of Walpurgis Mountain in Germany.

The roots of the Halloween we know and love in America today are tangled, but if you break it down into "trick" and "treat," it's a bit easier to trace, as David Skal does in his book *Death Makes a Holiday*. Skal says that by the time of the Renaissance in Europe, the idea of leaving "offerings" for the dead on All Saints' Eve was aligned with charity for the living. People begged and for their pains received, among other things, "soul cakes" made of oatmeal and molasses.

Another influence was the lavish masquerade balls held in the seventeenth century, during the reign of Charles I, to celebrate Hallowmas, which kicked off the Christmas season in England. These were a chance for the wealthy to show off their finery, but like May Day, Midsummer's Eve, and other English revels, they also encouraged an upside-down world where for one night everything—social order, gender, class—was in question and might even be its opposite.

By the nineteenth century in Great Britain and America, ideas about the returning dead had taken a back seat to fortunetelling games. The overriding goal was to identify your true love-to-be. A girl might carve an apple to pieces, then stand by a mirror displaying each on the tip of her knife before eating it.

With any luck, this summoned an apparition of her future husband, who dutifully appeared in the mirror. Apple "bobbing" or "snapping" is another game that at one time had a fortune-telling component. Not surprisingly, most of this merriment—whether apple bobbing or snapping or reading signs into cabbages and kale stalks pulled from the garden—made use of fruits, nuts, and vegetables, mining the theme of autumn harvest. People buried charms in mashed potatoes and parsnips: find a ring in your supper and you'd be wed within the year; find a thimble, you'd stay a spinster or bachelor; keys meant a journey, and coins promised wealth.

The pumpkin first showed up as a spooky symbol in American literature in Washington Irving's short story "The Legend of Sleepy Hollow," but the jack-o-lantern also draws on British folklore: the trickster Jack was so troublesome he was barred from both heaven and hell. The devil spared a single fiery coal to light Jack's wicked way until Judgment Day. Jack stowed his prize in a hollow turnip, using the handy "lantern" to lure travelers into the mire (this legend connects to another about Will-o-the-Wisp, the "fool's fire" or phosphorescent swamp gas that sometimes shines in the bogs of Britain).

These and many other games and stories crossed the Atlantic with the early settlers, and continued to reshape Halloween throughout the seventeenth, eighteenth, and nineteenth centuries. While pranks and trickery—an Irish and Scottish import, mainly—had always figured in, Halloween in Victorian America was a relatively well-behaved affair with private parties, matchmaking, and fortunetelling games like apple bobbing and candlestick jumping (*Ladies Home Journal* and other popular magazines published festive tips, just as Martha Stewart does today). But by the mid-1930s, U.S. homeowners weary of soaped windows started holding Halloween open houses complete with decorations, what Skal calls a "property protection strategy during the late Depression," and the custom of trick-or-treating was established. Children rang doorbells and fled, let the air out of tires, wrenched gates off their hinges, and hurled bags of flour at hapless passersby. Like the food offerings the Celts left their dead on the midnight conjunction of the old year and the new, treats and ornaments—acknowledgment—mollified young revelers with a glint in their eye and gave them pause.

Tribal people have often worn masks or otherwise ritually disguised themselves against evil spirits. The costume aspect of modern Halloween might reflect an ancient wish to camouflage ourselves, but the merry, topsy-turvy mood of Halloween implies we're as much modeling the wicked freedoms of these minions as concealing ourselves from them.

Skal calls the years after World War II "the glorious hey day of trick or treating," and from there Halloween "grew by leaps and bounds." It's the largest U.S. consumer holiday except for Christmas—with sales of candy, costumes, and decorations, and movie and theme park receipts reaping several billion dollars. The ancient ties to an autumnal festival may be a dim memory, but the primitive joys of getting to be absolutely anyone you want for one night remain.

See also: *Day(s) of the Dead.*

HAND OF GLORY

The Hand of Glory was the hand of an executed criminal, mummified and bleached for use in occult rites and ceremonies. The idea was that if you crafted virgin wax, Lapland sesame, and the fat from a hanged murderer into a candle, placed it in the mummified hand, and chanted incantations, you could go about your wicked work unseen. Burglars paid handsomely for a "dead man's candle," and as late as 1831, Irish thieves who were discovered raiding a mansion in County Meath were evidently using the demonic torch as their only source of illumination.

See also: *Superstitions.*

HAUNTING

Sightings of ghosts and ghostly activity or "hauntings" have been recorded throughout history. Those who die violently or in what is perceived to be an unnatural or disruptive way or whose bodies are not properly cared for after death are almost universally believed to be more vulnerable. Most ghost stories smack of tragedy. An untimely end leaves a spirit with unfinished business, wearily and sometimes detectably stuck between this world and that. The idea that hauntings often follow improper burial spans cultures. The ancient Assyrians had a word for the resulting apparition—an *ekimmu*—and a special rite designed to liberate *ekimmus* and send them on their way is preserved on a clay tablet. According to Suetonius, a Roman writer born in AD 69, all of Rome knew the insane Emperor Caligula haunted the Lamian Gardens after his assassination—until his sisters eventually gave him a decent burial.

After the December 26, 2004, tsunami claimed more than 215,000 lives in eleven countries around the Indian Ocean, leaving another 50,000 people unaccounted for, the coastal tourism trade in those areas fell off sharply, a fact many in the industry attributed to Asian tourists' fear of "hungry ghosts," agonized wayward spirits who lift food to their mouths only to have it morph into hot coals.

After the tragedy, many believed these *e gui,* or hungry ghosts, haunted seaside resorts and other affected areas—that those washed out to sea now walked among the living, eager to snatch others into spiritual limbo with them. Taxi drivers spoke of being hailed by Western tourists, taking them aboard, and finding the back seat empty when they reached their destination. Orange-robed monks were spotted on beaches sprinkling holy water or enacting cleansing ceremonies at wrecked hotels. One business owner who had suffered financial losses after abandoning a resort town said, "I don't want to go back. There are too many dead people there."

In 1860, as the American Civil War was beginning in earnest, Oliver Winchester became immediately and magnificently wealthy when his small company—soon to be known as the Winchester Repeating Arms Company—developed a devastating weapon that would radically alter the experience of battle. The magazine of the new Henry rifle could load and fire a bullet every three seconds.

Two years after the rifle debuted, Oliver's only son, William, married Sarah Pardee. They had and lost a child, and weathered Sarah's depression, but in 1881, William succumbed to tuberculosis, leaving Sarah widowed and alone at forty-two. She lapsed again into depression, turning for advice to a medium who soon claimed to make contact with her husband on the other side. William's report was grave: Sarah must use her not-insubstantial legacy to rinse clean the sins of the Winchester family.

Sarah continued to consult with the medium, and in 1892 purchased a farmhouse on 160 acres near San Jose, California. Thanks to a twenty-million-dollar inheritance and the private railroad she commissioned to deliver materials, the house grew at breakneck speed. More than six hundred rooms materialized and were torn apart again to make way for others. Sarah visited a séance room daily, and the spirits informed her what came next.

Not surprisingly, her charitable mission to oversee a spirit sanctuary for victims of the Winchester rifle eventually became a campaign to shield herself from spectral fury. To confound the spirits that plagued her, Sarah slept in a different room each night, selecting on a whim. She had dead-end doorways built. Stairways ended at walls, leading nowhere. The house continued to swell and shift form until her death in 1922, by which point it sprawled over six acres and boasted some 160 rooms, some of which were still under construction. The house is now a major tourist attraction.

Many alleged "hauntings" are faked, of course, to attract tourists or otherwise make a site more commercially appealing. Proprietors of historic houses, hotels, and restaurants mine existing stories and legends for their entertainment appeal.

Other hauntings are quickly explained by science.

Psychic investigators called to a "sighting" may scour old maps and books of local history for context and then interview everyone involved to ensure they're psychologically sound (and haven't been prescribed hallucination-friendly medication). Next they carefully examine the site, shoot photos and video, and make an accurate plan of the rooms, noting windows, mirrors, or anything in the vicinity that might affect the play of light or sound. Refractions, reflections, mist, and fog can all make ordinary shapes appear otherworldly. Ground vibrations caused by underground water movements may make objects "move" in a haunted house.

"Ghost busters" also measure temperature (a drop may accompany paranormal activity), often with an infrared noncontact thermometer, which reads the infrared rays emanating from an object (the more rays, the hotter the object). A magnetic field may also accompany ghostly manifestations, so investigators use an electromagnetic field meter (EMF) to measure a field's strength. Thermometers and EMF meters can also be connected to cameras, auto-firing when the temperature or magnetic field changes.

Not all hauntings involve visible apparitions. Inexplicable noises are more common: laughter, sobbing, music, footsteps, creaking, clanking, groaning, whistling. Usually materials expanding and contracting with changes in temperature are the culprits.

Different materials—metal, wood, brick—expand and contract at different rates. Sound is caused by vibration, so when materials shift and move against one another, you might be in for a racket. Renovation is another culprit. If you install an efficient new heating system in an old wood-framed house, for example, the wood may dry out and warp. To warp is to move is to vibrate is to sound off. Likewise, when a house "settles," or the ground begins to ever so gradually buckle under a building's foundation, the structure may complain with a creak or a groan.

The frequency of a sound is measured (in hertz) by how many waves pass a point every second. The human ear can detect a wide range of frequencies but not those that are very high or very low. Scientists have discovered that extremely low-frequency noise, below 10 hertz, can vibrate the eye's retina, causing a person to "see" objects that are not really there. See also: *Ghost.*

HEARSE

Today's hearse little resembles the horse-drawn vehicle that transported the dead in previous centuries. That vehicle was modeled on an earlier "herse" used by farmers in pre-Christian Britain: a large, heavy, usually triangular rake used to claw plowed ground smooth for planting. Flip this device over—with the spikes pointing upward—and you have the inspiration for the triangular hearse

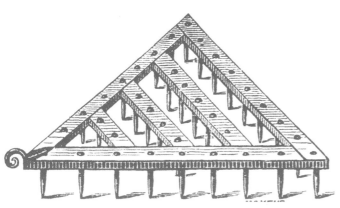

subsequently used in church services, its many candleholders mimicking the plowman's spikes. In time, this elaborate candleholder came to be associated with the vehicle that transported it together with the corpse to the grave, whether a fancy funeral coach or a shiny black Cadillac hearse.

HEART CASKETS

In medieval Europe, if a body couldn't be transported home for burial, survivors went to great lengths to save the heart. It was fashionable to bury it in a special casket, most often made of lead but also earthenware or, in the case of royalty, ivory or gold. The heart of Richard the Lion-Hearted, who died fighting in France in 1199, was returned to his beloved Rouen, and James II of England bequeathed his heart to a convent at Chaillot.

In the nineteenth century, the hearts of the poet John Keats, who died in Italy, and the explorer David Livingstone, who died in Africa, were shipped back to England for burial, while the heart of the poet Shelley was snatched from the funeral pyre by his friend, Trelawny, and sent to England.

HEAVEN

Heaven is generally thought of as a place where God or the gods dwell and where the souls of the devout go after death.

The Christian heaven is sometimes portrayed as a real destination for those who have achieved salvation—complete with halos, harps, pearly gates, and Saint Peter guarding those gates, admitting the righteous at his discretion. But for many believers, heaven is a metaphor meant to convey the bliss or ecstasy of dwelling in God's grace. It's a state of being rather than an actual address.

The Koran, the sacred scripture of the Muslim faith, depicts heaven as a paradise garden of immortality, shaded and crossed with rivers of milk and honey, wine and water—a place where believers enjoy refuge and bliss in the richness of God's mercy. Comfortably garbed in silk, the elect are never too hot or too cold. They relax on couches, sipping from silver goblets.

See also: *Judging*.

HELL

"All hope abandon, ye who enter here," reads the sign over the entrance to Hell in poet Dante Alighieri's masterpiece, *The Divine Comedy*, completed shortly before his death in 1321. Other world religions reference hell or hells—Hindu doctrine claims millions; Buddhists count from eight hells to thousands—and none of them are pretty; but neither do these non-Western versions house a soul eternally.

While modern Christian thought more often depicts hell as a state where God is absent, historically it's been painted (both literally and figuratively in myth and legend) as a fantastic underworld of cruelty, vice, and torment inhabited and overseen by demons and sometimes the Devil himself, its prince and premier sinner.

According to the August 28, 1990, issue of the defunct tabloid *Weekly World News*, hell is nine miles beneath the surface of a spot in western Siberia where Soviet engineers, drilling for oil, were forced to cap their hole after smelling smoke and hearing the cries of the condemned.

HEREAFTER

Is death the end?

Not according to the world's major religions, though you won't find the faithful agreeing on the nature and particulars of the next stage. Invariably the fate of the soul—whether bound for a certain destination or for a return to earth in changed form—depends on choices a person made in life.

The Assyrian, Babylonian, and Sumerian civilizations took a bleak view of the afterlife. Once you set off on the "the path that allows no journey back," you languished forever in a House of Dust or Darkness. There, according to *The Epic of Gilgamesh*, inhabitants ate clay and wore birdlike coats of feathers.

The ancient Egyptians expected the next life to look a lot like this one. They preserved and entombed the corpse, sometimes with a model double so that if the body decayed, the double could journey on to the other world. With proper spells and planning in life, the Egyptian became an *akh aper*, or "equipped spirit,"

and wore protective amulets. They also worshiped the sun, making up to twenty thousand human sacrifices a year to fuel its voyage across the sky and repay what they saw as a debt to the gods, who had sacrificed themselves to create the earth, moon, stars, crops, and humans. Aztec heaven had thirteen levels guarded by one-hundred-plus gods, and where you ended up had more to do with how you died than with how you lived. Those who drowned or were struck by lightning, died in war, in childhood, or as a sacrifice each lit out for a special heaven or region of heaven. The ordinary dead, meanwhile, inhabited a dreary if uneventful underworld called Mictlan, ruled by the Lord of the Dead.

After a one-way boat trip across the River Styx, the average citizen in ancient Greece or Rome anticipated eternity in Hades, yet another gloomy, sunless underworld. A fortunate few, mostly heroes, enjoyed perpetual bliss in the Elysian Fields or the Isles of the Blessed.

Old Norse heroes crossed the Rainbow Bridge to spend eternity in Valhalla, which had many of the same benefits as the Elysian Fields, and in old Ireland, graves were barrows or burial mounds called *sids*, where both the dead and their ancient gods, the Tuatha Dé Danann, resided. So a Celt might simply remain in his grave, weapons and belongings by his side, or he might inhabit a Valhalla-like underworld where dead warriors fought on, often rising to do battle the very day after they died.

after death, traveling to one of several afterlife destinations. (Egyptian faith focused on the sun and the sun god Ra, and just as the sun moved from dawn to dusk to night, so the soul might move, inhabiting different realms.) The soul itself was no single entity but had several aspects, including the *ka,* or body double, a sort of guardian spirit after death, and the *ba,* the soul as it appears on earth after a person dies, usually depicted as a bird with a human head.

Like the Egyptians, the Aztecs built pyramids, believed in spells and magic,

The Old Testament refers to Sheol, a place very like Hades as the Greek poet Homer saw it, with the dead hanging on as bloodless shades: "For to him that is joined to all the living there is hope: for a living dog is better than a dead lion. For the living know that they shall die: but the dead know not any thing, neither have they any more reward; for the memory of them is forgotten. Also their love, and their hatred, and their envy, is now perished; neither have they any more a portion for ever in any thing that is done under the sun" (Ecclesiastes, 9). But the view of modern Judaism is probably more in line with King Solomon's assertion that "The dust will return to the ground as it was, and the spirit will return to God who gave it" (Ecclesiastes 12:17).

Christianity offered a wide selection of destinations for the soul, including heaven and hell, purgatory, and formerly, limbo.

Islamic martyrs suffer no judgment. Those killed in a holy war, or who perished in defense of their beliefs, are excused their sins and sent straight on to the paradise gardens. But most Muslims anticipate a complex series of events after physical death, all relating to the state of the soul in life.

Hindu ideas about the afterlife focus on karma, the moral law of cause and effect, a kind of balance sheet of sin and virtue. The "self," or *atman,* is born and reborn through many lifetimes, with outcomes in each determined by karma.

Like Hindus, Buddhists believe in reincarnation and karma—if not in the individual soul. For them there is no such thing as a "self," an unchanging, personal energy that moves from body to body. The Buddha taught that a person is like a stream of flowing water, with the majority of that stream ceasing in death. Only the karma continues on. One life follows another like the turning of a wheel until a soul achieves nirvana, which means "to be extinguished" or released from longing, attachment, and suffering.

Many tribal societies imagine two distinct afterlife destinations, but up isn't always heavenly and down isn't always hellish. The Inuit believed in both an Underworld and a Sky World, and for the Greenland Inuit, the sky region was cold and food was scarce, so down below was the better bet. The Tlingits of the Northwest Coast positioned the dead in an underworld far away to the north but in the sky also, where the souls of those killed in warfare battle on as the northern lights.

Many cultures have the living and the dead in constant interaction. The Dieri of Southeast Australia position the spirits of their dead in the Milky Way, and though it's an agreeable place, the dead at times depart the "River of Sky" to visit the living, often in dreams. For Australian Aboriginals, the human spirit exits the body in death and journeys in ghostlike form to a new life in the land of the dead, where it joins the ancestors who came there in the Dreaming. Often described as the "sky country" or "cloudland" to the west, it is furnished with plenty of water and game. Life is as it was, only better. The spirit can return to wander the bush, enjoying leftovers and deserted campfires, and the living can encounter them in waking dreams. Aboriginal doctors may visit the land of the dead to solicit advice or wisdom.

In African religions, the dead are contacted, honored, and called on for help. There are many "classes" of the dead in traditional African belief, all very much alive in the minds and daily routines of the living.

See also: *Ancestor worship, Book of the Dead, Consciousness, Cryonics, Grave goods, Hades, Hell, Heaven, Limbo, Mummy, NDE, Purgatory, Sin eating, Soul, Spiritualism, Valhalla.*

HORROR MOVIES
(ALSO *SLASHER MOVIES*)

Death never strays far from the characters in fright flicks. Why do we like to see people in harm's way (or worse)?

From early classics like *The Cabinet of Dr. Caligari* to *Nosferatu,* based on Bram Stoker's *Dracula,* to gory cult picks like *Night of the Living Dead* and *Texas Chainsaw Massacre* and modern classics like *The Shining* and *Alien,* horror movies help us face our fears and step away safely. After all, the world is violent and scary sometimes. We may value rational self-restraint as the established norm— if we're good and law-abiding, we're often taught everyone else will be too— but the daily news doesn't always support that view.

Horror movies may temporarily relieve our fears and anxieties about society and the unknown. They also let us play out our own instinctive aggressions within accepted bounds. Like bungee jumping and roller coasters, blood and suspense can be fun; it gets your adrenaline pumping. But we're talking prescribed fun contained in a dark theater for a span of ninety minutes. The boundaries are clear, and things tend to be resolved by the end, which may trigger for viewers a feeling the ancient Greeks called "catharsis," a purging or release of strong emotions like fear.

Many horror movies dance with or around death, but slasher or "body count" films—critic Roger Ebert calls them "dead teenager movies"—bump and grind with it. This horror subgenre features a (usually) masked psychopathic killer who stalks and systematically butchers young adults, especially

those testing out sex or illegal drugs. In a back story, we learn why said violent psycho favors said methods in said location on said anniversary. The teen cast may rally and try in vain to shoot, burn, electrocute, drown, or otherwise dispense with the killer, but these attacks only render the fiend more mythic and promise a sequel (a promise often honored many, many times).

Alfred Hitchcock's thriller *Psycho* first introduced the disguised maniac with a freaky pedigree and a knife, and its famous shower scene was a defining moment in cinematic history, but it isn't a slasher movie in its own right (too few victims, for one thing).

Slasher movies peaked in the late 1970s and '80s with blockbusters like *Halloween, Friday the 13th,* and *A Nightmare on Elm Street* and were more recently revived and parodied in films like *Scream* and *Scary Movie*.

HOSPICE

When doctors diagnose someone as terminally ill, their treatment changes. The goal is no longer to cure a person but to ease suffering and make the patient comfortable. At this stage, a patient may opt to leave the hospital. A hospice is a small facility or home dedicated to caring for and supporting the terminally ill.

Most hospices have a patient-centered philosophy and a holistic approach to medicine. While hospice staff use drugs to treat pain, nausea, and other symp-toms, they also help a dying patient come to terms, spiritually and emotionally, with the inevitable. Hospice care provides for the needs of not only the dying patient but that person's family and can be given at home as well as in a formal facility.

HOUDINI

Legend has it that before his death on October 31, 1926, the great magician and escape artist Harry Houdini vowed he would perform the ultimate feat: he would elude death itself. Houdini societies the world over still convene yearly on Halloween to conduct séances with hopes of contacting him, though no one has succeeded yet.

Houdini credited some of his most famous tricks to Ira Davenport, an internationally acclaimed Lily Dale spiritualist and medium, but later became one of spiritualism's chief enemies. In *Houdini: A Magician Among the Spirits,* he admitted that with age—and in light of his own experiences with grief—he realized "the seriousness of trifling with the hallowed reverence which the average human being bestows upon the departed." The showman who had once deceived others said: "I was chagrined that I should ever have been guilty of such frivolity and for the first time realized that it bordered on crime. . . . I became deeply interested to discover if there was a possible reality to the return, by Spirit, of one who had passed over the border and ever since have

devoted to this effort my heart and soul and what brainpower I possess."

Houdini began a "new line of psychical research," making a pact with fourteen different people: whoever died first would make a point of communicating with the others. He brought together one of the largest libraries in the world on psychic phenomena, with material dating back to 1489, and read everything he could find on modern spiritualism. He staged an energetic campaign to expose fraudulent mediums and methods like slate writing and spirit photography. Mediums, Houdini argued, made promises they couldn't keep and claims they couldn't prove. They preyed on the gullible and the grieving, and their "religion" had become a source of suffering, of "crimes and atrocities." Resident spiritualists evidently so feared Houdini's visits (he was known to infiltrate séances in disguise) that they often hid behind locked doors.

In the end, he had to conclude that "deluded brains" were behind all the phenomena he had investigated. "In thirty years I have not found one incident that savored of the genuine."

See also: *Lily Dale, Medium, Spiritualism.*

JUDGMENT (OF SOULS)

Many faiths hold with one or another form of final judgment, and some imagine an actual graveside or after-death trial to settle the fate of the soul.

The ancient Egyptians believed that the dead person entered the Hall of Two Truths, where the jackal-headed god Anubis weighed his or her heart on a scale against cosmic order, or *Ma'at,* represented by a feather. If they did not balance, Ammut—a female demon with the head of a crocodile, the body of a lion, and the backside of a hippopotamus—sat to the right of the scales, ready to devour the wretch. If the heart and feather balanced, he/she was led into the presence of Osiris, god of nature and fertility, who waited on his throne. Before this ruler of the dead and more than forty other divine judges—including the individual's *ba,* which served as a witness—the deceased denied wrongdoing. Only when the gods were satisfied could the spirit enter a serene afterlife with Osiris in the Field of Reeds, which was a perfected version of Egypt where the dead enjoyed abundant harvests.

In Tibetan tradition, Yama, the king of truth, oversees a formal hearing once a spirit seeking union with the Absolute has weathered a forty-nine-day intermediate state. At the trial, the spirit's good and evil deeds are placed on either side of a scale judiciously held by the Monkey-Headed One. Gods serve as prosecution and defense and otherwise watch the proceedings to keep them impartial.

Both Judeo-Christian and Muslim traditions refer to a day of judgment or "reckoning" at the end of time, when God judges the moral worth of individuals or the entire human race.

In Islamic tradition, a person is intensely aware of what transpires after death, both in flesh and in spirit. Released from the body by four angels in white, the soul shimmers like a drop of mercury in one angel's hand. Roughly the size of a bee, it holds its human aspect, watching with great grief as loved ones mourn and prepare the vacated body for burial. The soul suffers a horrible thirst, but to accept a drink is to for-

The Dome of the Rock, built during the Umayyad caliphate (seventh century BC) on the Temple Mount in Jerusalem. The arcade in front of the Rock is called the Scales. In Muslim tradition, this is where the scales for the weighing of souls will hang on Judgment Day.

sake salvation, and should the soul pass this test, angels escort it to heaven, knocking at the door to each of seven levels of paradise and announcing the deceased there, together with a person's sins and virtues. The evil are barred from the seven heavens and hurled back to earth. The virtuous are admitted into the holy presence of God.

In some interpretations of the Koran, the soul is sent back to the grave to await the end of time and must also undergo a *fitnat al-Qabr,* or gravesite trial, con-ducted by the angels Munkar and Nakir. Described as black with green eyes, the angels—who appear terrifying to the wicked—test the soul on the tenets of Islam. Those who answer correctly enjoy sweet-smelling breezes, the breath of paradise, as their graves expand; those who fail are overwhelmed by heat and smoke, the breath of hell, and their graves contract and crush them.

In either case, this temporary "second life" hints at what's to come.
See also: *Karma.*

KARMA

This Hindu rule of cause and effect governs life and rebirth: what you contribute to the universe comes back to you; if you live a good and pure life, you earn good karma and a favorable rebirth. Bad actions win you the opposite. Most people endure a period of reward or punishment before being sent back to assume another form, and the morally bankrupt may face incarnation as a non-human animal or insect.

We're all subject to *samsara,* a relentless wheel of birth, death, and rebirth, and the final goal of Hindu spirituality is to achieve *moksa,* liberation from the wheel.

See also: *Hereafter, Reincarnation.*

LAST REQUEST

In books and movies, a character's dying request is treated with grave solemnity. To ignore a final wish or final words may cost you; it may even curse you.

Even today, most condemned prisoners get the last meal of their choice. Four-time murderer Dennis Bagwell, executed by lethal injection in Texas in 2005, called for a beefsteak with A1 Sauce, six pieces of fried chicken, barbecued ribs, two hamburgers, a pound of fried bacon, a dozen scrambled eggs, French fries, onion rings, salad with ranch dressing, peach cobbler, ice tea, milk, and coffee.

When asked in 1960 by the commander of the Utah execution team if he had a parting request, murderer James W. Rodgers—one of the last people condemned to die in the United States by firing squad—evidently quipped, "Why, yes. A bulletproof vest, please."

On a more positive note, the Make-a-Wish Foundation makes every effort to treat children faced with life-threatening illness to their hearts' delight. Founded in Arizona in 1980, the foundation claims to grant a wish "every forty-one minutes" and now has chapters all over the world. The first child to make a wish was a seven-year-old boy who wanted to be a policeman. Officers from the Arizona Department of Public Safety fitted him with a uniform, helmet, and badge, and took him for a spin in their helicopter.

His joy inspired other compassionate people to follow suit, and a grass-roots organization was formed that is today one of the world's best-known charities, supported by a network of more than twenty-five thousand volunteers and funded almost entirely by public and corporate contributions and foundation grants, including individual donations of hotel rooms, transportation, and meals. The Make-a-Wish Foundation not only supports sick children but offers hope and strength to suffering families, helping to offset the pain and stress of illness.

LAST RITES
(OR *EXTREME UNCTION*)

A sacrament administered by both the

Eastern Orthodox Church and the Roman Catholic Church requesting forgiveness of sins. For the "last anointing," a priest dips his thumb in sanctified oil and makes the sign of the cross on the person's eyes, ears, nose, lips, hands, and feet. Then the priest recites in Latin, "Through this holy anointing and by His most tender mercy may the Lord pardon whatever sins you have committed . . . by your sight, by your hearing, by your hands . . ."

See also: *Funerary rites.*

LAST WORDS

Those slated for execution have long been expected to deliver choice words before the hangman or firing squad does the deed. England's Newgate Prison, which hosted many an execution, kept an official "calendar" or "Malefactor's Bloody Register" in which authorities recorded the last words of traitors, highwaymen, murderers, and thieves. Sometimes printers made up and distributed handbills before or after the execution. The Newgate Calendar is no single volume but various and sundry collections spanning nearly two centuries and sporting titles like *The Newgate Calendar or MALEFACTOR'S BLOODY REGISTER containing: Genuine and Circumstantial Narrative of the lives and transactions, various exploits and Dying Speeches of the Most Notorious Criminals of both sexes who suffered Death Punishment in Gt. Britain and Ireland for High Treason Petty Treason Murder Piracy Felony Thieving Highway Robberies Forgery Rapes Bigamy Burglaries Riots and various other horrid crimes and misdemeanours on a plan entirely new, wherein will be fully displayed the regular progress from virtue to vice interspersed with striking reflections on the conduct of those unhappy wretches who have fallen a sacrifice to the laws of their country.* This particular edition, for the years 1774–78, was housed in three volumes.

See also: *Capital punishment, Music.*

LIFE EXPECTANCY (ALSO *LIFE SPAN*)

The projected length of time that a person will live (if all goes as it should), or life expectancy, is not the same as life span, how long that person actually *does* live.

Through all but a fraction of history, human life expectancy fell roughly between 18 and 20 years of age. It only rose to 33.5 years as late as the seventeenth century, and then only in Europe. In 1640, the average person lived to be 32. More than a quarter of all children failed to reach their fifteenth birthday, and only about 5 percent of the population made it to age 60. Death usually happened at home, in public, with relatives, friends, and a minister by the sickbed. Immediately after World War II, the life expectancy of the average U.S. citizen at birth was just 66.7 years.

The U.S. average life span right now is about age 75 for men and age 80 for women, though drugs being developed to treat disease are also, according to a 2007 article in the *Economist,* enhancing the "cognitive powers of healthy people and pushing human life expectancy much further," perhaps to well beyond 115 years.

Transhumanists—a loose collective of scientists, technologists, and thinkers committed to enhancing the human condition—welcome these innovations. Why not conquer death one day if we can do it? Human nature, says Nick Bostrom, an Oxford University philosopher and advocate of transhumanism, is "a work in progress, a half-baked beginning that we can learn to remold in desirable ways . . . we shall eventually manage to become post-human, beings with vastly greater capacities than present human beings have."

See also: *Causes of death, Eternal life (quest for).*

LIGHT

Some Orthodox Jews burn a lamp for twenty-four hours on the anniversary of a loved one's death, while on All Souls' Day devout Catholics light votive candles. In the Scottish lowlands, the oldest survivor in the family of the deceased waves a lighted candle three times over the corpse before sprinkling it with salt. In Kyoto, on the last day of Obon, symbolic fires burn on mountaintops to lure lingering spirits back to the afterlife. On islands along the Inland Sea, families make small paper boats, set them ablaze, and watch them float out to the night sea, twinkling to darkness.

An eternal flame burns at the grave of John F. Kennedy and at the site traditionally believed to hold Christ's tomb in the Church of the Holy Sepulchre in Jerusalem. These and other ritualistic uses of candles, lamps, and flame are holdovers from a time when people hoped to light the dark path the dead must travel to the next world. Light helped the living, too; fire in any form was a sure way to ward off evil spirits tempted to take charge of a body left vacant. Even in most modern U.S. funeral parlors, lights burn all night in the chapel where a corpse lies.

See also: *Funerary rites.*

LILY DALE

Founded more than 120 years ago, Lily Dale, at a glance, is a quaint Victorian hamlet in western New York. One of the first upstate communities to score electricity, its official (and metaphorical) nickname is "the City of Light," but it may be better known as "the town that talks to the dead" since some twenty thousand guests crowd through its gates annually to confer with spiritualist mediums. In the summer season there are dozens of resident mediums to choose from (and each has passed a rigorous test before being invited to hang out his or her shingle).

Pilgrims flock to Lily Dale each summer in search of sympathy and healing, out of curiosity, or just for fun; but mostly they come with hopes of encountering someone or ones on "the other side."

The historian Ron Nagy displays a spirit trumpet at Lily Dale Museum.

In the lobby of Lily Dale's Maplewood hotel, a sign cautions against conducting séances and circles in public rooms. Tourists testify over morning coffee, swapping tales of wandering spirits, knocks and noises in the night, shifting furniture. Visitors convene outdoors daily by "the stump" at the Forest Temple, where mediums spot eager visitors from the Beyond hovering by living relatives—and "serve spirit" by delivering messages to the audience.

Lily Dale has a long, colorful history. Screen star Mae West was a devotee of a medium named Jack Kelly and a regular in his parlor. Suffragette Susan B. Anthony was another frequent visitor—though not a spiritualist herself—and in legend at least, when a medium fielded a message for her from an aunt, she replied, "I didn't like her when she was alive, and I don't want to hear from her now."

Early spiritualists were staunch advocates of progressive political causes like female emancipation, but today the focus is more generally educational and recreational, with sweat lodge ceremonies and New Age workshops on topics like Reiki, self-realization, "Dreams and Astral Travel," and "Painting with the Spirits" among the offerings.

See also: *Fox sisters, Houdini, Medium, Spiritualism.*

LIMBO

The term means "fringe" or "edge" and in Catholic dogma referred to the state of or place for those souls—primarily the souls of unbaptized infants—who did not deserve the punishments of hell but could not be admitted into heaven or purgatory until Christ cleansed them of original sin.

In 2007 the Vatican determined that limbo does not exist. "The many factors that we have considered," wrote the International Theological Commission, a Vatican advisory board, "give serious theological and liturgical grounds for hope that unbaptised infants who die will be saved." The medieval concept of limbo as a place where they would spend eternity without communion with God, the document states, seems an "unduly restrictive view of salvation."

See also: *Heaven, Hell, Purgatory.*

MARTYR

A person becomes a martyr when his or her death is used to sanctify a deity, defend a cause, or prove a point. Jesus of Nazareth, Socrates, Gandhi, and Oscar Romero, who cared for the poor in El Salvador and was murdered after alienating those who exploited them, are very different examples.

See also: *Assassination.*

MEDIUM

A medium is a person who claims to communicate with the dead through psychic or paranormal means. Different mediums draw on different methods. Some are clairvoyant and work visually. Others are clairsentient or clairaudient and rely on their intuition or hearing. Trance and materialist mediums enter altered states of consciousness, allowing spirits to communicate through their voices, features, and gestures, or even bodies (via a rather unsavory-looking item called ectoplasm, the tangible substance cre-

ated from the energy field surrounding the spirit).

Spirits too have different means or preferences for being in touch, using the medium as a conduit or intermediary. Some employ automatic writing, guiding a medium's hand—and a pen or pencil—over paper, which results in handwriting very different from the medium's. Other spirits or guides reveal themselves in drawings or "spirit" photographs made by the medium's hand.

Many mediums conduct séances. These may or may not still involve table tipping, a method wherein people hold hands across the table while one among them poses a question. Spirit energy surges through participants' hands—very lightly placed on the special three-legged table—and reportedly makes the table tip or move. Through one or another tedious translation methods comes the answer to that query.

For "trumpet circles," a medium places a special metal horn in the middle of the circle as the group focuses hard on attracting spirit energy. If a spirit consents to join them, the trumpet rises in the dark and begins to sound.

The notorious séances of the early 1900s were as much about entertainment as outreach, but many spiritualist mediums today see the séance as a valid way to "lift the veil" and communicate with those in the other plane.

See also: *Fox sisters, Houdini, Lily Dale, Spiritualism.*

ELLEN BOURN codirects and teaches at the Northeast Academy of Healing and Psychic Development and has been a registered nurse and psychiatric counselor in the Buffalo area for more than twenty-five years. She is also a life member and current president of the Lily Dale Assembly, the largest spiritualist community in the world.

If you had to sum up the core messages of Spiritualism, I asked her, *how would you do it?*

Belief in the continuity of life. You do have a spirit or soul, and communication between all planes of existence is a reality. Mediumship and healing are gifts. Also, spiritualism believes in personal responsibility rather than vicarious atonement.

So these spirits on the other side are benevolent? They want to help?

Now you're getting more into spiritualist philosophy. Message work is healing. We're not into negative spirits.

So it isn't a random thing? Spirits aren't just "coming through"?

You need to know how to work with spirit; that's part of being a medium. If somebody was an unaware person and a "jerk" on the earth plane, just because they pass over three days later, do they suddenly become a genius? I don't know the answer to that, but I do know that what you send out is what you attract. So if you send out for the benevolent spirit, that's who comes to you. Why would you want the other ones?

You know how teenagers like to play with a Ouija board and usually don't know what they're doing? Let me ask you . . . if you just open up a table or a board and say, "Okay, whoever's out there, come on in and have a conversation," who do you think you're getting? Have you thought about how many there are on the other side?

I tell people, "Do me a favor: when you go home, open your front door and make a pot of coffee, and the very next person who walks past your house, whether you know them or not, let them in for a cup."

You wouldn't do it over there, so why would you do it here?

When you work with spirit, you have to ask for those coming in white light. Some people say a little prayer, and then call in the spirit they want to speak to. If you send a message out—that you have a concern—people there may want and choose to answer it.

MEMENTO MORI

AS. SOONE. AS. WEE. TO. BEE. BEGVNNE:
WE. DID. BEGINNE. TO. BE. VNDONE.

—inscribed on an English memento
mori medal, c. 1650

The approximate translation here is "Remember you must die," or "Remember to die," and in the Middle Ages, a memento mori was an impersonal reminder that death comes to all, be they beggar or king. The idea found its way into architecture and art but was also applied to simple objects and trinkets: a human skull doubling as a paperweight, a miniature silver coffin, an ivory and gold skeleton timepiece inscribed with "As I am, so must you be." Less a tribute to a particular person than acknowledgment of our universal mortal plight, these objects were set on a writing table

and pondered. Memento mori still resonate today in the folk art, skull-shaped candies, and bread adorned with crossed "bones" available during the Mexican Days of the Dead.

See also: *Dance of death, Day(s) of the Dead, Mementos, Plague.*

MEMENTOS–FOR THE LIVING (AT FUNERALS)

In England and colonial America, mourners often received gifts when they attended funerals, including scarves, gloves, ribbons, or lace of black or white. Wealthy families might even provide gold rings to the more important mourners. These often depicted a skull or were engraved with some suitable inscription in English or Latin, such as "Behold the End," or *Dominus abstulit,* "The Lord has taken away."

MEMENTOS–OF THE DEAD

Even when a death has receded into memory, survivors seize or seek some trace or token of the departed, a keepsake, a lock of hair, a letter. I once saw a photograph of an early-twentieth-century widow in the Andaman Islands wearing her husband's skull on a cord around her neck; but for many, the need to memorialize is satisfied by a certain photograph or a simple mass card. Other mourners wear the clothes of the departed to feel close to them, to hold on to their smell, their essence, a little longer. Too much finality too quickly can be wrenching.

Today in the West, we're squeamish about death. We like it sanitized and kept at bay, but our ancestors simply couldn't have ignored it. In the United States between 1650 and 1750, for instance, parents might expect one in every four children to die. People took ill, died, and were laid out in their homes. Rural pioneer settlers buried them in the backyard.

Perhaps because death was ever near at hand, people hung samplers on their walls embroidered with the names and death dates of family members. They slept under "crazy" quilts pieced together from the clothes of the dead—bits of mourning clothes, wedding gowns, even shrouds—stitching in symbols of their lives together: flags, ships, hearts, stars, verses both consoling and sorrowfully resigned. This impulse is reflected today in the AIDS quilt, with which an entire society seeks to honor and remember.

The nineteenth-century Victorians even went so far as to make a fashion statement out of remembering their dead. In 1847 you could bring hair clippings—"a piece of thee"—to London's fashionable Regent Street, where an "artist in hair" would braid it into a tasseled necklace with a gold clasp. A few years later, someone devised a brooch called the "swivel" with two glass boxes that swiveled to reveal hair on one side and a tiny portrait of the departed on the other. While intimate, hair also resists decay, and Victorian mourners had it fashioned into everything from lockets to watch chains.

Victorian mourning bracelet with a band of woven hair, c. 1865.

Since only the very wealthy could commission formal keepsakes like death masks, tomb effigies, memorial statues, or portraits, the invention of photography made it possible for nearly everyone to have a likeness of a loved one, resulting in a fad for photographing the dead.

Victorian women carried small glass vials called "tear catchers," and whenever they wept with sorrow over a loved one who was gone, they would catch their tears in the bottle to keep as a memento.

Today some people are having the carbon removed from the ashes of cremated loved ones and turned into diamonds. A company named LifeGem will turn "cremains" into yellow or blue diamonds—your choice of round, princess, or radiant (rectangular) shape, certified by a gemologist from the Gemological Institute of America. The process that creates these gems may be artificial, but the gems, apparently, are not. Each receives a grade for size and brilliance and is priced accordingly—from $2,500 to $14,000 for diamonds ranging from a quarter to a full carat.
See also: *Deathbed portraits, Memento mori.*

In this
as in the heart
for whom he s
the memory of
is enshrin

MEMORIAL

For thousands of years people all over the world have marked the final resting place of their dead with buildings, gravesites, statues, or other structures, both in remembrance and as a way of honoring them. The marker may be as simple as a rock-pile cairn or as complex and gigantic as the pyramids the Egyptians built for their pharaohs. Mostly, though, it's something in between. Stone markers last for centuries. In the far north, wood, which decays slowly in cold climates, may be used. Sometimes the dead are placed under or inside structures such as mausoleums and spirit houses.

Some memorials are not permanent objects but temporary alterations to the landscape in tribute and remembrance, a mark of public mourning, such as raising a flag at half-mast.

Since the early twentieth century, grief in Western culture has been largely a private and invisible affair, but every now and then, in little altars at the side of the road marking the site of fatal car accidents, we see public expressions of love and loss contained in plastic flowers and weathered teddy bears.

Sometimes, too, a catastrophe like the Oklahoma City bombing in 1995, the 9/11 destruction of the World Trade Center, or the tsunami of 2004 takes so many human lives that whole societies mourn, expressing their collective grief through impromptu memorials such as candle altars on traffic islands or flowers heaped by public walls under posted poems and photos. The news brings us very close to these tragedies, even if no one we know has been directly affected, perhaps because they remind us of our own mortality and that of those we love.

MEMORIAL SERVICE

A ceremony held for a dead person when the body is not present.
See also: *Eulogy.*

MIRRORS

Mirrors have always had symbolic ties to the soul. They were often covered when a death took place, not so much out of enforced modesty to squelch wrongful vanity, but because it could prove dangerous for the spirit to glimpse its reflection or be given access to a likeness of the living.

Some Bombay Muslims carry out these rites earlier, during illness, concealing every mirror in the house to spare an invalid the sight of his or her own reflection, which might otherwise be absorbed into the mirror.

In medieval Europe, people turned the mirrors in a house to face the wall after a death for similar reasons; the mirror might catch and hold a reflection of the dead, and that reflection could also radiate out again, spreading death like contagion.

The idea that you earn seven years' bad luck (or worse) when you break a mirror originates here as well: to harm your reflection is to harm your soul.
See also: *Mourning, Water.*

MONUMENT

We construct monuments for our dead both diligently—by hiring professionals to craft lasting stone markers for cemetery plots or war memorials for city squares—and spontaneously, in popular tribute, such as the intimate handmade memorials and simple crosses that sprout at roadsides after car accidents or the spray-painted walls of remembrance that appear in urban neighborhoods wracked by street violence. Either way, a monument is for viewing. It's a public offering, one that speaks of a grief shared.
See also: *Memorial, Shrine.*

MORGUE

A morgue is simply a place where corpses are kept until they are claimed or released for burial.

MOURNING

When death separates us from people we love, we feel many things: shock, denial, confusion, depression, panic, grief—even guilt or anger. In time, with support, we can find our way to acceptance. We need both "protection from painful experiences and the boldness to face them," author and physician Elisabeth Kübler-Ross has said. "If we choose to love, we must also have the courage to grieve."

They don't call mourning a process for nothing, and as we master all those heavy feelings and the hollowness they leave behind, it helps to have the comfort of established practices and formulas.

Societies all over the world have created rituals that honor the dead and consecrate their passage—even as they help survivors with their own passage through grief.

selves on the corpse, and beat their foreheads with stones till they bleed. Once the fire begins to dry out the body, the display of intense sorrow begins to wane. Several days later, when the corpse is entirely dehydrated, it's set in a place of honor. The Dani people distribute the deceased's property among the community at large.

The Tiwi of Australia may go so far as to arrange a new husband for the widow, who then marries at the funeral. The Bara of southern Madagascar lay out the body in a "house of many tears," where women weep for three days. Separated by daylight, women and men gather only at night to feast, drink rum, sing, and dance. In Indonesia, families wait several years to cremate loved ones, enough time to save funds for elaborate funeral feasts.

In many cultures, people made a living selling their services as professional mourners or keeners. This tradition can be traced back to ancient Egypt, Mesopotamia, Greece, and Rome, though more recent variations occur in Ireland, Africa, and elsewhere.

Nearly every culture sets aside a prescribed period for mourning, a time for friends and family to comfort and care for a bereaved household, though the length of time varies.

Hindus consciously limit this time to thirteen days after cremation, as prolonged mourning might hold the dead back from their journey. Jewish mourners sit shiva for seven days, followed by a less restricted period called *sheloshim*, ending thirty days after a death. The

In North America today, mourning is a mostly private and more or less invisible act, but many traditional societies view it as a natural part of the life cycle and a community event. In New Guinea, the Kaluli of Papua New Guinea gather en masse to sing mourning songs, while the Kukukuku mummify their deceased relatives by smoking them over a fire. The ceremony begins with four days of mourning, during which relatives wail and tear their hair, eat dirt, throw them-

Japanese mark the seventh day after, as well as the one-month anniversary and the forty-ninth day, when the transition to the spirit world is thought complete. The stage of heavy mourning for Muslims, during which finery and certain foods (sugar in coffee, for instance) are prohibited, ends after forty days.

Washing and preparing the body; helping to shovel earth onto the coffin, light the pyre, or otherwise participate in a funeral; making and sharing food; wailing and tearing hair or clothing; withdrawing from certain aspects of workaday life—these and many other elements recur all over the world, at all points in history, and clearly speak to something deep in the human condition.

Every society has its mourning "etiquette," the established dos and don'ts that reflect how it feels about death at any given time in any given place.

Ancient and medieval attitudes, which might be matter-of-factly summed up as "To everything there is a season" and "Death comes to all," were softened in the nineteenth century by the Christian model of a happy heaven—and the idea that loved ones would be reunited there. Death was "so long" but not "goodbye," a temporary separation. Mourning became an art form under Britain's Queen Victoria, the model "loyal" widow. After Prince Albert died in 1861, she mourned in near seclusion for years and wore black for the remaining forty years of her life. The Victorians saw mourning as a critical component of a good society, marking loss and shunning pleasure for years. They instituted rules and stages of dress—a formal progression from black crepe to black to gray to white and lavender—and schedules for when it was acceptable to start wearing jewelry again or attend dinner parties.

Children of the day were not sheltered from the rites and practices of mourning. In the decades before the American Civil War referred to as the antebellum period, older children wore black or crepe for six months after the death of a parent—three months of "full" mourning, with a gradually diminishing degree of black from there on (known as "half" mourning). Children under twelve wore white in summer and gray in winter, and their suits were trimmed with black buttons, belts, or ribbons. Even infants were trimmed in black.

All this changed in the early twentieth century. Faced with the carnage of World War I, people came to see excessive mourning like Queen Victoria's as morbid or antisocial. The sooner the bereaved reentered society, the less pronounced, less present the loss would seem. Social pressure urged a brisk return to normal life. Mourners should "stay occupied," resist burdening others with private woe. To grieve had become a selfish act.

But by the early 1960s, when the personal and political overlapped and "feelings" were there to be discussed, the tide had turned again. In her seminal book *On Death and Dying*, Elisabeth Kübler-Ross interviewed terminally ill cancer patients and brought death and mortality out into the light again, inspiring a whole genre of self-help books on grief and healing.

Today the tide appears to be in yet another "ebb" stage. The scientific quest for eternal youth—whether through cryonics, genetic enhancement, or chemical peels—has once more landed death low on the list of acceptable discussion topics. We like to keep it out of sight, preferring to believe that science has us on the brink of immortality. Will the passing of that large and socially influential segment of the population known as the "boomers" trigger another shift?

MOURNING—ALTERING APPEARANCE IN

Many societies mourn their dead by cutting or otherwise altering their clothing, their hair, or their faces and bodies.

Mourners wore red in ancient Rome, as it evoked the blood drawn when women scratched their faces at funerals. Some Indian tribes gashed their faces, arms, hands, and legs in grief. When Prince Alfonso of Portugal died in 1491, Princess Isabel cut her hair, wore only sackcloth, and refused to undress for forty days; Portuguese men cut their hair and beards, and women scratched their faces bloody.

The Dani people of Irian Jaya selected a prepubescent girl from the tribe and sent a healer the morning after a cremation ceremony to accept her sacrifice. With a swift blow from a stone adz, a finger was amputated up to the second

George Catlin (1796–1872), *Mah-to-toh-pa, Four Bears, Second Chief in Mourning (Mandan)*, 1832. Oil on canvas. Smithsonian American Art Museum, Washington, D.C.

joint and thrown onto the dying embers of the funeral fire, after which the child's hand was bandaged with banana leaves.

On Bathurst Island, north of Australia, Tiwi mourners paint their bodies and cut and burn their hair at funerals. Tiwi believe dead spirits are lonely and try to take their friends and family with them. Mourners are in a state of *pukimani,* or spiritual danger, and must disguise themselves.

In many cultures such as rural Greece, Italy, and Mexico, a widow conceals herself by wearing black for many years, possibly even a lifetime, and might avoid her husband's grave so that his spirit will not wander back to her. In like fashion, a Palestinian widow may cover the bright coins in her headdress, which reflect her wealth and marital status.

Because hair in many societies is a symbol of virility, life, and sexuality, a widow's may be cut or shaved. Hindu widows in Bengal and Madras once had their heads shaved, as did Igbo widows in Nigeria.

Other societies, including many North American tribes, display sorrow by cutting the hair of both sexes. The Haya people in Tanzania shave their heads in mourning but only then; an otherwise shorn head looks like a death wish.

Some societies veer the other way and forbid the cutting of hair. During the Qing dynasty, Chinese men couldn't shave their heads for a hundred days after an emperor died. Bereaved men in New Caledonia stop cutting their hair and sport turbans made of bark.

See also: *Funerary rites, Mourning, Mourning dress, Mourning warehouses, Shrines.*

MOURNING DRESS

After his first voyage to New Zealand, Captain James Cook noticed that Maori widows wore wreaths of rushes and bird feathers, sometimes decorated with bird bills and heads.

In nineteenth-century Europe or North America, you had no other reason to wear elaborate, scratchy black crepe garb—or one of the black armbands that emerged as an acceptable substitute if you couldn't afford formal mourning clothes—than to say: *Somebody close to me has died.* Though anthropologists might argue that the idea of "fading to black" originated in our wish to conceal our-

selves from the spirit of the dearly departed, mourning clothes mark us. Among the living, they set us apart as vulnerable and serve as a plea for lenience, patience, understanding from the world around us. *Tread softly,* they urge. *This person is hurting.*

Often these clothes are plain, sober, modest. They discourage vanity. Observant Jews in mourning wear slippers instead of formal leather shoes. In twenty-first-century China, people may mourn in clothes of coarse, undyed hemp.

In the Taoist, Buddhist, and Confucian traditions, death is the gateway to rebirth—a theoretically joyous occasion—so the Chinese and other Asian cultures have traditionally worn white. Hindus also favor white; some Gypsy tribes choose red; Armenians and Syrians wear light blue.

So while black is the norm in Western society and just seems to fit the mood, it's by no means the universal color of mourning.

See also: *Funeral rites, Mourning, Mourning warehouses.*

MOURNING WAREHOUSES

Mourning warehouses—what the French called *maisons de noir,* or black houses—were actually the first department stores. Middle-class Victorians had strict rules for what to wear and how to behave while mourning. All but the most destitute, it was understood, should follow a particular code of dress—even small children, who were mostly clothed as

mini-adults until the second half of the eighteenth century anyway. Mourning houses began to appear in the 1840s to satisfy the clamor for "black goods," and the bigger houses, such as Grande Maison de Noir in Paris, or the House of Jay in London, offered true one-stop shopping for the bereaved. That is, everything from the hearse to an etiquette book to guide your household through the process.
See also: *Mourning, Mourning dress.*

MUMMY

Ancient Egyptians created the first human-made mummies. They believed the soul left the body at the time of death but reunited with it in the next world. They preserved the body against decay so the soul would recognize it.

According to Herodotus, an ancient Greek historian who visited Egypt, there were three different procedures for turning a person into a mummy, depending on how wealthy a family was, or wasn't.

If the family of the deceased had wealth, embalmers removed everything inside the corpse except the heart—which the mummy-in-transit would need in the judgment phase—and washed the body with palm wine and spice. Next they covered it with natron, a form of sodium carbonate or natural salt, for seventy days. Lastly they rubbed the body with cedar oil, natron, and gum; stuffed it with sawdust, sand, or wads of linen; and wrapped it in layers of linen bandages. The not-so-rich rated a more streamlined version of the same process, while the poor just had their intestines flushed out and their bodies left in natron for the requisite seventy days.

Egyptian coffin panels have revealed still more about the process of preparing a body for the next life, depicting masked priests leading sacred rituals while the hollowed body dried in its bed of natron or was wrapped, and, beneath the bier, jars holding the mummy's internal organs.

The Egyptians weren't the only ones to practice the art of embalming. The Paraca Indians in what is now Peru used sophisticated embalming techniques. The Kukukuku of Papua New Guinea mummified their deceased relatives by smoking them over a fire, and in Japan huge candles were used to smoke dry the corpses of certain Buddhist priests to venerate them.
See also: *Embalming.*

MURDER

(OR *HOMICIDE*)

The biblical commandment "Thou shalt not kill" has long been overlooked. Intentional, unlawful killing of one person by another has been on the human record at least since Cain and Abel, sons of Adam and Eve—who in Christian dogma were the first man and first woman. Cain slew Abel out of envy and resentment, and since then all manner of motives have inspired murder—not least power, passion, and money.

According to the U.S. Uniform Crime Reporting Program, about 14,990 persons were murdered in the United States in 2005—roughly 5.7 murders per 100,000 inhabitants—and of those reporting a motive, 26.1 percent were triggered by "arguments (including romantic triangles)."

While serial killers take the lives of several victims over a span of time, mass murderers kill many victims at once, in one place, as in the Columbine High School and Virginia Tech massacres.

Traditionally many societies viewed murder and other forms of premature death as upsetting the natural order of things. These acts are a crime against nature, and to restore the order, many communities historically managed the bodies of murder victims differently, laying them to rest with exceptional care and caution. Several tribes of the Dakota, who would normally carry out a scaffold or air burial and then inter the remains in a second burial, might bury the bodies of murder victims in the ground at once,

face down, with a piece of fat in the mouth. Without such an offering, nature might punish the imbalance by removing game from the area. Burying the body face down also disoriented the spirit and kept it from finding its way back to seek revenge. In the folklore of many cultures, a life ended prematurely unleashes a restless spirit, so steps must be taken to make that spirit content.

See also: *Appeasing the dead, Assassination, Forensic science, Genocide, Ghost, Haunting, Serial killer.*

MUSIC

From dirges to death metal, spirituals to bagpipe laments, music has always helped us master grief, or at least manage it; given us a means of expressing how we feel about death and dying; and complemented our death rites.

Berawan villagers of Long Jegan in Borneo use drums and gongs to instruct the soul in its passage to the next world, and U.S. slaves drummed in Congo Park, New Orleans, to send spirits of their dead back to their ancestral land.

Many funeral planners still favor Chopin's "The Funeral March" from the third movement of Piano Sonata no. 2 in B-flat Minor, opus 35, or George Frederick Handel's "Dead March" from the oratorio "Saul." Mozart, Verdi, and other classical composers wrote famous requiems, pieces originally meant for the liturgical Mass for the Dead, in the eighteenth and nineteenth centuries.

Music thanatologists, who provide

music-based therapy for dying patients and their families, hold "vigils" in which a harpist or handful of musicians visit and play music selected to soothe and shift a patient's focus from ongoing pain, worry, and fear.

Death has always traipsed through traditional ballads. These narrative songs originated in the oral tradition but by the mid-1600s were being printed around Europe for popular consumption. Urban printers adapted old ballads and penned new ones steeped in folklore or the daily news. They narrated the lives and exploits of aristocrats and Bible characters and outlaws like Robin Hood, told of great floods, fires, and battles, and announced local news with street vendors hawking cheap "ballad cards" to commemorate sensational crimes, especially murder.

Printed broadside ballads—"slips" or "slip songs" as they were called—were the forerunners of modern pop music. They first appeared in the New World not long after the earliest Europeans came, so ancient songs from the Scots Highlands, for example, got to take new root in settings like the Appalachian Mountains. But death, particularly of doomed or unrequited or forbidden lovers, remained a favorite theme in tunes with haunting names like "Sweet William's Ghost."

Contemporary folk and rock balladeers like Johnny Cash, Kate Rusby, Bruce Springsteen, Nick Cave, and the Decemberists have drawn on all of these influences, evoking ghost lovers of old and crafting murder ballads for a new age.

See also: *Goth, Mourning.*

THE UNQUIET GRAVE

"The wind doth blow today, my love,
And a few small drops of rain;
I never had but one true-love,
In cold grave she was lain.
I'll do as much for my true-love
As any young man may;
I'll sit and mourn all at her grave
For a twelvemonth and a day."
The twelvemonth and a day being up,
The dead began to speak:
"Oh who sits weeping on my grave,
And will not let me sleep?"
"'Tis I, my love, sits on your grave,
And will not let you sleep;
For I crave one kiss of your clay-cold lips,
And that is all I seek."
"You crave one kiss of my clay-cold lips,
But my breath smells earthy strong;
If you have one kiss of my clay-cold lips,
Your time will not be long."
"'Tis down in yonder garden green,
Love, where we used to walk,
The finest flower that ere was seen
Is withered to a stalk."
"The stalk is withered dry, my love,
So will our hearts decay;
So make yourself content, my love,
Till God calls you away."

—Traditional ballad

NATURAL DEATH MOVEMENT
(ALSO *SIMPLE DEATH*)

Helping families arrange affordable, privately organized, environmentally friendly funerals while improving the quality of dying are the goals of the natural death movement and its death centers, which offer midwives for terminally ill patients, death exercises, and recyclable coffins.

Founder Nicholas Albery reported in the London *Guardian* newspaper that his idea came from natural childbirth. It occurred to him that "there could be that same feeling of expectation, of transition, as at birth. Dying could be an ecstatic experience." The Natural Death Centre that he founded with his wife and a fellow psychotherapist offers exercises and rituals to help people ready for death emotionally, reduce their anxiety, and die at home if they choose.

Ernest Morgan's *Dealing Creatively with Death: A Manual of Death Education and Simple Burial* offers do-it-yourself diagrams for constructing a simple burial box out of fiber or plywood. He also suggests the following, if a loved one has asked to have his or her body donated to science:

The family may prefer to take the body to the medical school themselves, using a station wagon. This has been the practice in our family, and we would not think of turning it over to someone else. It is something we can do for the loved one and helps us to accept the loss. The body may be placed in a box on a stretcher or plain canvas cot, or simply wrapped in a blanket. People are repelled by death and often shrink from handling a dead body. In practice, however, the privilege of helping to care for the body of a friend or a loved one is a deeply meaningful experience. Too often in modern life we withdraw from reality or call in a professional to do things we might benefit by doing for ourselves.

See also: *Burial—eco, Funerary rites.*

NEAR-DEATH EXPERIENCE (NDE)

Some people who survive heart attacks and other life-threatening events report having looked down on their own bodies while medical teams worked to revive them. Many ventured into a dark tunnel toward a bright light and were greeted by dead relatives and friends or other benevolent figures cloaked in light. Most experienced a feeling of bliss or overwhelming peace.

Near-death experiences, or NDEs, perplex researchers because they shouldn't be possible. Not according to what we know about the brain. Simultaneous recording of heart rate and brain output reveals that within eleven to twenty seconds of heart failure, the brain, starved of oxygen, shuts down. A flat electroencephalogram (EEG) recording indicates that the brain has ceased functioning at this point, and yet, it's in this period between switch-off and resuscitation, say researchers, that NDEs most often occur. Many patients describe heightened perceptions and clear thought processes, and form memories, at a time when the brain is technically not capable of coordinating activity.

One of the more persuasive NDEs on record is the case of Pam Reynolds, an American who underwent brain surgery for an aneurysm in 1991. In preparation for her procedure, Reynolds's eyes had been taped shut; her ears were blocked; to ensure that her brain was functioning on only the most basic level, her EEG was carefully monitored. And yet when Reynolds came to, she described not only a full-scale NDE but the bone saw that had been used to cut her skull.

Researcher Pim van Lommel, a retired Dutch cardiologist who now studies NDEs full-time and lectures all over the world, challenges the very idea that memories are localized in the brain. "In my view, the brain is not producing consciousness, but it enables us to experience our consciousness," he says. NDEs imply that consciousness can be experienced in an alternative dimension without "our body-linked concepts of time and space." He compares the brain to a TV, which receives programming by decoding information from electromagnetic waves, though it isn't generating that content.

The long list of celebrities who have reported NDEs or elements thereof include singer Tony Bennett, rock legend Ozzy Osbourne, and actors Chevy Chase, Sharon Stone, Peter Sellers, Donald Sutherland, Lou Gossett Jr., Jane Seymour, Elizabeth Taylor, and Gary Busey.

NECROMANCY

Use of the dead or of objects relating to them in ritual magic was staunchly prohibited in the Bible. Deuteronomy 18:9–13 says those who practice it and traffic "with ghosts and spirits . . . are abominable to the Lord."

All the same, Israelites like Saul—with help from the witch of Endor—invoked and consulted the "shades" of Sheol in times of crisis, and necromancy was com-

The scholar John Dee and necromancer Edward Kelly conjure up a dead man.

mon practice among all levels of society in medieval Europe, never mind the real and present threat that one might be accused of witchcraft. The cult of saintly relics is its own form of necromancy.

Many cultures held that with proper ritual protection the energy, strength, and vitality of the dying or newly dead could be captured and absorbed by the living, bringing luck and longevity. Ancient traditions from Central Asia and China to Egypt, Africa, Mesopotamia, and Central America carried out ritual human sacrifice, as did the ancient Celts, Greeks, and Scandinavians. Funerary cannibalism is another variation on this theme. As recently as the 1950s, a New Guinea tribe called the Fore engaged in the ritual consumption of the dead, a practice that led to an epidemic of kuru or "shaking death," a neurodegenerative condition that resembles mad cow disease.

In medieval England, people believed the touch of a still-warm corpse cured illness and disease, which made for groping crowds at packed public executions.

After a body had been left to the elements for "sky burial," Tibetan Buddhists might make ceremonial musical instruments of human thighbones and ritual caps of skulls.

The human head has been an object of necromancy in many cultures. The ancient Celts believed the protective power of dead heroes survived even death and lined up the heads of their fallen warriors on hillsides to greet approaching enemies.

Renowned for their head-hunting and -shrinking techniques, the Jibaros of South America believed the soul lived in the head, so to seize, shrink, and adorn yourself with the head of an enemy was to absorb their portion of spiritual power.

Human sacrifice is yet another means of assuming the strength and virility of the dead or dying. Aztec religion revolved around human sacrifice, and in the fifteenth century alone, some 250,000 victims were sacrificed annually. Many ancient cultures from Chinese to Mesopotamian to Egyptian sacrificed the servants, wives, children, and pets of important citizens, burying them together to provide company and continued support in the next life.

Romans and, later, Europeans were intrigued by the funerary rites of the Egyptians—ancient and mysterious even then—and got the notion that swallowing a powder made from mummified corpses would heal what ailed them. Not surprisingly, entrepreneurs began ransacking Egyptian tombs and grinding up the good inhabitants to supply the demands of fashion. There weren't enough tombs to go around, though, which inspired a trade in fake "mummy powder."

See also: *Mummy, Saintly relics, Serial killers, Undead.*

NIRVANA

The story of the Buddha assumes an almost mythic or legendary character in the telling, but modern scholars agree that the historical Buddha (circa 563–483 BC) was a young prince who attained perfect enlightenment after leaving home some 2,500 years ago to embark on the life of a wandering ascetic.

Unknown, *Death of Buddha.* Prince Siddhartha Gautama (c. 563–c. 483 BC), founder of Buddhism, on his deathbed.

Twenty-nine-year-old Prince Siddhartha's sheltered life ended abruptly the day he ventured out of his palatial home and saw a decrepit man stooped over a staff. In his innocence, the prince begged his chariot driver to explain.

"Old age," whispered his companion. "It comes to all."

Similarly shaken by the sight of a sick man and a dead body, Siddhartha grasped the painful truth that death, too, must one day come to all.

But as luck would have it, the next figure he glimpsed was a holy man, serene in yellow robes. Inspired, the prince renounced his life of ease and wandered out into the miseries of the wider world. He embarked on a path of mystical study in search of the peace he had witnessed that day in the monk.

One morning, seated cross-legged under a fig tree, Siddhartha resolved to remain there until he could escape the eternal wheel of birth, death, and rebirth.

At length he grasped the "four noble truths"—all lives, whether of beggar or king, are defined by misery; misery comes of craving; craving can be abolished; to do so, you follow a methodical path of moderation and mindfulness—and he achieved enlightenment.

The spiritual goal of Buddhism is not an afterlife in paradise but a state of inner freedom; nirvana is final liberation from the cycle of death and rebirth and from the yoke of craving or desire, a "blowing out" of the ego.

See also: *Reincarnation.*

OBITUARY

At one time, writing death notices or obituaries—working the "dead beat"—for a newspaper was thought of as grunt work, an entry-level stop for those looking to a future in journalism. Today the form is recognized and respected, and many writers achieve celebrity status writing graceful, empathetic, and carefully researched biographical obituaries of famous subjects.

News services like the Associated Press may keep prewritten obituaries of notable people on file, updating as and when appropriate. Obituaries can be vital historical records and personal tributes, and many organizations urge their members to draft their own notices in advance.

The *New York Sun* obliged showman P. T. Barnum by printing his obituary early, two weeks before his death in 1891, so he could savor it. The headline read: "Great and Only Barnum—He Wanted to Read His Obituary—Here It Is."

◆ ◆ ◆

ORGAN DONORSHIP

Can the dead help the living? In 1982 there were 103 heart transplants in the United States. In 1999 that number jumped to 2,185. Both the United States and Canada have growing resources and guidelines for those interested in donating their organs, but demand still outpaces supply.

In *Dealing Creatively with Death,* Ernest Morgan cites "21,692 life-saving organ transplants in the U.S. [in 1999]—kidneys, livers, pancreases, intestines, hearts, and lungs. But the waiting list of patients in June of 2000 numbered 70,240. In short less than a third of the people in the U.S. who need organs, and who qualify medically for transplants are able to receive them. Tens of thousands of them die needlessly."

Almost everyone is a potential donor. While younger people are preferred for major organs, people over sixty may donate corneas, middle ear tissue, bones, and skin. Tissue transplants include skin grafts for critically burned patients, donated corneas help avert or correct blindness, and donated bone, cartilage, and tendons aid reconstruction and rehabilitation. You can also leave your entire body to a medical school to help train future doctors and dentists.

The Uniform Anatomical Gift Act of 1968 (AGA), which has been adopted to some degree by all fifty U.S. states, has encouraged more people to make anatomical gifts by regulating the laws and guidelines for doing so. The AGA provides a wallet-size donor card, signed by a person over eighteen and witnessed by two other adults, that legally permits physicians to remove organs after death.

OSIRIS

The ancient Egyptians weren't so much obsessed with death as they were sworn to life. They wanted to see it go on, and all their death rites—mummification, entombment, and ritual remembrance—were designed with that end in mind.

The god Osiris played a key role in their belief system. Once a king on earth, he was slain by his jealous brother Seth, who carved his body into fourteen segments, scattering them around Egypt. His wife, Isis, gathered all but the heart—which was consumed by the greedy crocodile god, Sobek. Together with the ibis god, Thoth, and jackal-headed Anubis, Isis fitted the body back together, creating the first mummy. But Isis could revive Osiris only long enough to conceive an heir, Horus. After that Osiris had to return to the underworld, and became ruler of the dead.

The spiritual goal of the Egyptians was to spend eternity in the Field of Rushes, where the blessed harvested rich crops under the beneficent eye of their lord Osiris. At first only pharaohs had this opportunity—and symbolically "became" Osiris in the underworld—but eventually the promise of eternal life opened to all. To achieve it, ritual care had to be given to all the elements that make up a complete person: the physical body, the name, the shadow, and the *ba* and *ka*, which together are the equivalent of what we call the soul.

Many tombs contained "Osiris beds," wooden frames in the form of Osiris, filled with soil and sown with seeds of barley as a promise of new life to come. See also: *Embalming, Mummy, Soul.*

PALLBEARER

A pallium, or pall, is the heavy, sometimes ornamented cloth draped over a coffin, so the term "pallbearer" came to mean the one who carries or attends the coffin. Close family members or friends tend to do the honors of bearing the coffin to and from the hearse for religious services and burial, and they are usually male: brothers, uncles, sons, fathers, and husbands of the deceased. In Jewish custom, a personal enemy—attending as a form of regret—may also participate.

PLAGUE

In his book *Outbreak: Plagues That Changed History,* Bryn Barnard writes, "You're born pristine and alone, but it doesn't last. With your first independent breath, your body becomes a cooperative venture with other creatures: a colony, a host."

Barnard goes on to relay how from birth we're infested with tiny microbes we can't see, single-celled bacteria mostly, delivered by the air, water, and food we consume and by everything we touch. The average adult carts around some two pounds of microbes in her stomach.

Is this as unpleasant as it sounds? No. Many microbes are symbiants, meaning they work *for* us as well as in and on us. They keep our bodies in balance by doing everything from helping us digest food to grooming our eyelashes.

Some microbes do not help us. They're opportunists, inhabiting us at our expense as parasites. If enough people live closely together under the right (or wrong, as the case may be) conditions, an infectious microbe or pathogen can range widely through a population, resulting in an epidemic. An especially virulent disease can overtake a continent and grow global in scope, at which point we call it a pandemic. If the pathogen settles into a region as a permanent fixture, we call it an endemic.

Infectious diseases like bubonic plague, smallpox, cholera, tuberculosis, influenza, yellow fever, and, more recently, AIDS can utterly decimate and transform a society, and fear of such killers runs deep.

WE ALL FALL DOWN

Some scholars believe the bacterium *Yersinia pestis,* carried by rats and transmitted to humans through fleas that feed on the rodents' infected blood, should be implicated in the fall of the Roman Empire, but by the fourteenth century its ravages were largely forgotten.

A. Bjcklin, *The Plague,* 1898.

A succession of natural disasters in the 1330s—drought, flooding, famine, and finally earthquakes, which disturbed endless quantities of rats, some of which likely bore bubonic plague, and put them on the move—triggered new outbreaks in China.

In the fourteenth century, China (which takes up one-fourteenth of the land surface of the globe) was a remote and insular kingdom. Many people still traveled it on foot, so the new plague laid low for a while. By 1346, though, it had made its mark on most of Asia. It dipped into the Middle East, inching along the silk roads and up the Tigris from Baghdad, through Armenia to Italian trade stations in the Crimea. Here it hitched a ride back to Italy, France, and Germany, touching down in England in early 1348, with London reporting cases as early as November.

People must not have known what hit them. The first symptoms appeared suddenly. Body temperature rose to about 104 degrees Fahrenheit, with vomiting, muscular pain, and delirium. Freckles or skin blotches appeared, and the lymph nodes throughout the body—especially those in the armpits and groin—swelled and filled with pus. (These excruciatingly painful "buboes" gave the bubonic plague its name.) In about 90 percent of cases, the victim died within days.

Because popular wisdom had it that the pestilence spread on noxious vapor or the stench of putrefying corpses, people wore or carried nosegays of roses or lined their pockets with the "posies" cited in the familiar nursery rhyme later and perhaps erroneously linked to the disease. Sneezing could be an early indicator that the disease had struck ("Atchoo!" in the nursery rhyme was corrupted to "Ashes!," though many variations exist, from "Tisha!" to "Ah-Tishoo!") And soon, very soon, those who had contracted the disease fell down dead. Some contemporary reports had victims nodding off at night without any symptoms at all, only to be uncovered in the morning as decaying corpses.

⊕

Ring a ring of rosies,
A pocket full of posies
Atchoo! Atchoo!
We all fall down.

⊕

London doctors, those who hadn't fled the stricken city while they had the chance, wore a surreal costume: armor or a waxed-linen robe over a chalk-powdered shirt, a wide-brimmed hat, gloves, and a leather mask with glass or crystal lenses and a long beak filled with vinegar-soaked cloth and spices to offset the stink of death. (Imagine looking up through fevered eyes at that.)

The most common treatment was bloodletting, but other cures of the day included poultices of human excrement, a medicine made of diced snake, treacle, and wine, or, for the wealthy, powdered emeralds. Boiled meat and eggs were stricken from a patient's diet, and a safe night's sleep involved alternating from right side to left to regulate heat in the liver.

These treatments were not the eccentricities of a few physicians but common practice, the fruits of orthodox medical training of the day. The study of internal anatomy was all but disabled when Pope Boniface III—faced with an exploding black market trade in religious "relics"— issued a papal bull in 1300 forbidding the mutilation of corpses.

The Black Death decimated Europe, killing 75 million people: between a quarter and a half of the continent's total population. Though the Black Death was a well-documented case, lethal epidemics have not been confined to the Middle Ages. An influenza outbreak in 1918 killed more people in a single year— upward of 12.5 million—than the First World War that preceded it.

In May 2007, a lawyer from Atlanta, Georgia, became an alarming focus of international attention when the news broke that he had flown to Europe for his wedding with a rare and virulent form of tuberculosis resistant to most available drug options. Though Centers for Disease Control and Prevention (CDC) officials advised him to remain in Rome, where he was honeymooning, Andrew Speaker and his wife traveled to the Czech Republic, flew to Montreal, and drove back into the United States in a rental car. As health officials around the world scrambled to locate some eighty passengers who had been seated within five rows of him on two transatlantic flights, the CDC placed Speaker under involuntary isolation (similar to quarantine), slapping him with the first CDC isolation order since 1963.

Health officials later revealed that Speaker's strain of TB was more treatable than had originally been thought, but in July, nine fellow passengers from the Prague-to-Montreal flight filed a $1.3 million lawsuit against Speaker—by then dubbed "the TB guy" and "TB Andy" by the media—for potentially exposing them to the disease.

PLASTINATION

Dr. Gunther von Hagens's patented method of preserving a dead body substitutes an infusion of acetone and plastics for bodily fluids. Cured with heat, light, and gas, the plastinated cadaver is odorless, decay-resistant, and pose-able. The doctor has toured Body Worlds, his collection of recrafted human bodies and body segments, in twenty-six cities around the world and has evidently been inundated with offers from future donors.

Body Worlds shows specimens in ordinary and athletic motion: kicking a soccer ball, pondering a chess move, shooting hoops. Exhibiting both anatomical form and function, the animated, lifelike poses reveal, among other things, the organs and tissues in action. See also: *Embalming, Mummy, Taxidermy.*

POSTMORTEM PHOTOGRAPHY

Almost as soon as photography was invented in the early nineteenth century, it was used to record the dead, from tintypes of grieving mothers cradling dead infants to portraits of extended family grouped around an open coffin in the yard. Today the idea of reminiscing over

"postmortems" or pictures of dead people gives us the willies, but we also take imagery—print, electronic, animated—for granted. We're inundated with it.

Kodak put snapshots within the reach of ordinary families in the 1890s, but before that, if you didn't have someone in your household who could draw, or the money to hire a professional artist, you risked ending up without a single likeness of a person you loved. The idea that somebody dear really had departed forever—leaving behind loved ones with no means of remembering the deceased's singular features—must have been beyond difficult.

In many deathbed portraits, subjects appear to be sleeping peacefully, though a telltale rose or lily with snapped stem in their grasp might hint otherwise. Memorial portraits of mourners without the body present were also commonplace.

Postmortem photography evolved along with society's attitudes about death. In the 1870s, a more utilitarian sort of record began to eclipse the artful early generation of postmortems. Funeral directors called them "beautiful memory pictures" and seized the chance to show off fashionably padded and trimmed coffins (now called "caskets" in the United States—after a word for jewelry boxes, to position them as receptacles for precious cargo).

Mainstream demand for memorial photography decreased in the 1920s when many of today's attitudes about death began to emerge.
See also: *Deathbed portraits, Death masks*

PURGATORY

In Catholic doctrine, your average sinner proceeds to purgatory after death. Here the soul is purged and refined, perhaps over the course of hundreds or thousands of years, and gradually purified enough to ascend to heaven. Purgatory, a sort of "between" for the unsettled soul, offered an explanation for how ghosts, which most people in the Middle Ages and before believed in, could wander the earth. It also explained what transpired in the space of time between the individual soul's judgment and the ultimate or Last Judgment.

Early Catholics took for granted that almost everyone—apart from saints and martyrs or the irredeemably wicked, who were dispatched to hell directly—had to pay their dues in purgatory. The prayers of the living, the Church taught, could aid the dead and ease or shorten their stay.

PYRE

A pyre is a structure or pile of open-air combustible materials used to burn the dead. In India, the wood-fueled pyre is an everyday sight, but in the United States and other countries, a stream of natural gas is the more likely method. Some Buddhist traditions feature beautifully decorated cremation towers that serve as pyres, and the whole tower burns with the body.
See also: *Cremation, Funerary rites.*

REINCARNATION

"As a man leaves an old garment and puts on one that is new," says the Bhagavad-Gita, a Hindu sacred poem, "the Spirit leaves his mortal body and then puts on one that is new."

In Hindu belief, a person's soul, or *atman,* is reborn many times before it can cycle back to Brahman, the essence of the universe. Hindu sacred scripture teaches that while bodily forms were created, souls were *emanated* by Brahman itself, meaning they're part of that larger cosmic principle. So every soul journeys back to its source by way of a great many births, deaths, and rebirths, with behavior in this life helping to decide what earthly form—from lowly insect to Brahmin (a human with exalted spiritual status)—a person takes in the next.

Many cultures believe in reincarnation, but the concept of rebirth may be most commonly associated with the Tibetan Dalai Lama. Exactly forty-nine days after the death of a Dalai Lama, it is believed that his spirit is reborn into the body of a male infant. Through mystical inquiry, high lamas and others familiar with the Dalai Lama in his last life embark on a full-scale search to identify their new high priest. When they locate a likely candidate, they may test the child by laying out an array of objects to see if he can pinpoint those belonging to the late Dalai Lama.

In many traditions, new parents looked for signs that their baby might be a one-time family member returned to them. If the Vikings found a birthmark or other telling sign, they named the newborn after his or her predecessor. The Yoruba of West Africa often named a baby boy Babatunde, meaning "Father has returned," and a baby girl Yetunde, "Mother has returned."

See also: *Karma.*

RELICS

In medieval Europe, people swore by the magical properties of saints, holding even their skin and bones in reverent awe. A dead saint's body might be ripped asunder by faithful Christians craving miraculous healing. Everything from boots to finger bones were ferreted away to accommodate the sick and needy, with neither tooth nor scrap of garment remaining. Corpses of famous saints were dismantled and divvied up among rival churches, which put these "relics" on display. The underendowed even attempted to steal relics from competing churches to boost their reputations.

The tongues of a number of saints were said to remain intact long after their bodies had decayed. Housed in a special reliquary, Saint Anthony of Padua's was pronounced "red, soft and entire" more than four hundred years after his death. Visitors to St. Mary's Catholic Cathedral in Edinburgh can view a shoulder blade of Scotland's patron saint, Saint Andrew.

Draining off and venerating saintly fluids for the sake of miracle making was common practice in AD 305 when Saint Januarius, an Italian bishop, died. Blood was extracted from corpses hours (allegedly even years!) after the death, with witnesses blotting it up in garments to soak up luck and protection. Some of the blood of Saint Januarius,

who lived and died seventeen centuries ago, is kept in a small vial in the Cathedral of Naples. Most days it looks dark, dry, and solid, but every so often—usually several times a year—it miraculously liquefies, turning purple or bright red. Though critics claim the liquefaction could be triggered by the deliberate addition of a thixotropic gel, such as hydrated iron oxide, which decreases viscosity when agitated, thousands turn out each year to witness what they fully perceive to be a miracle.

But it isn't only saintly relics that have captured the imagination of the public.

In 1987 Chinese archeologists unearthed a treasure-filled crypt in an ancient temple seventy miles from Xian, the home of the famous terracotta army. Among the riches were a series of Chinese boxes, made of iron, sandalwood, rock crystal, and jade. Inside the latter was a mildewed finger bone that had evidently been quite precious to the rulers of the Tang Dynasty (AD 618–906). Whose bone was it? The Buddha's, according to an inscription on the outer box.

When the great twentieth-century scientist Albert Einstein died in 1955, his body was cremated. His brain, however, was preserved at his request for post-mortem study. Einstein wanted to help researchers get a handle on how the brain works. More than twenty years later, a journalist let on that while much of Einstein's precious gray matter had been sectioned and sent to specialists around the country, the remainder had been "filed" in an old cider carton in the corner of pathologist Dr. Thomas Harvey's office.

In the 1980s, a glass tube containing four hairs from the imperial head of the emperor Napoleon sold for 280 pounds at a Sotheby's sale in Monte Carlo. The covert "bone trade"—what a dealer interviewed in *Cabinet* magazine called an "international market in corporeal collectibles"—is still brisk today, serving a public in search of "contact with a dead person through a living artifact." This dealer dubs skulls, eyes, fingers, brain matter, and blood "the Big Five" and says he organizes his own offerings "first by physical category . . . and then by historical or cultural categories— American presidents, movie stars, Nazis, outlaws, and so on."

See also: *Autopsy, Body snatching.*

RESURRECTION

Christianity adopted the ancient Hebrew idea that Adam and Eve earned death as the "the wages of sin." Their fall from grace cost them—and all humanity— immortality.

In Christian belief, Jesus of Nazareth was crucified and killed by the Romans, and rose three days later, appearing to some of his disciples before ascending to heaven. His death, then, was a sacrifice that rinsed away the sins of believers, who in turn gain salvation and resurrection through Christ at the Last Judgment. "And God shall wipe away all tears from their eyes," says Revelation 21:4, "and there shall be no more death."

Hebrew, Christian, and Muslim doctrines all promise that believers will rise from the dead at the Last Judgment or day of final reckoning at the end of time.

But it's not only religion that vows to undo death. As the French philosopher and writer Voltaire observed during the Enlightenment, "Everything in nature is resurrection." So perhaps, inspired by cycles and seasons and relentless organic patterns, we've tried and failed for centuries to follow nature's model, treating dead bodies with everything from herbs and potions to electric shock.

Many a cautionary tale has been told about the potential side effects of "playing God" or tempting fate, from W. W. Jacob's "The Monkey's Paw" (1902) to Stephen King's *Pet Sematary* (1983). Failed nineteenth-century efforts to ply the dead with electricity, which must have seemed intriguingly far-fetched at the time, inspired Mary Shelley to write her classic gothic novel, *Frankenstein*, about a monster pieced together from parts and shocked to life by a bolt from the blue— only to wreak havoc on humanity.

Today, people whose hearts have stopped, who might on the face of it

seem "dead," are revived all the time. Among the methods used to rouse the heart are defibrillator paddles, which start blood pumping again by sending electric shocks to the heart muscle.
See also: *Cryonics, Judgment, Near-death experience, Necromancy.*

RIGOR MORTIS

Soon after an animal dies, its muscles relax and grow limp. Over the next few hours, oxygen starvation triggers a chemical reaction in the muscles, making them seize up and stiffen. This rigidity, or rigor mortis, lasts for a day or two before the muscles start to relax again.

Liver mortis happens when the heart stops pumping blood through the body and—thanks to gravity—settles in the areas of the body nearest the ground. This buildup, or pooling, causes discoloration of the skin, or lividity, which looks like severe bruising.

SARCOPHAGUS

The word derives from ancient Greek and Latin terms for "flesh-eating stone"—in honor of a kind of limestone used at the time for coffins and credited with consuming the flesh of corpses. Today, we think of a sarcophagus as a freestanding stone container for a body, usually inscribed or decorated and displayed as a monument. Inside their sturdy stone sarcophagi, royal mummies in ancient Egypt were often nested within one or many coffins.

The tenth duke of Hamilton, who died in 1852, commissioned a tremendous and costly mausoleum in Scotland meant to showcase an Egyptian sarcophagus he'd picked up for the then princely sum of eleven thousand pounds. Unfortunately, the Egyptian the sarcophagus had been designed for was a good deal smaller than the duke, whose noble feet had to be severed from his outsize corpse and buried separately.

SERIAL KILLER

The official FBI definition of serial murder is "three or more separate events with an emotional cooling-off period between homicides, each murder taking place at a different location." This cooling-off period is what sets a serial killer apart from a mass murderer.

Not a few early serial killers were aristocrats. After Joan of Arc's execution in 1431, her noble compatriot Gilles de

Rais, who earned high military honors during the Hundred Years' War, spiraled into a nine-year-cycle of vicious savagery during which he stalked the children of local peasants, torturing and dismembering his victims. Known as the "bestial Baron," he was executed in 1440, and some believe he was the model for the fairy-tale villain Bluebeard.

The seventeenth-century countess Elizabeth Bathory—convinced the lifeblood of virgins was an elixir of youth—spilled and bathed in the blood of as many as 650 servants and other young women in her native Hungary before she was found out.

Historically, grisly murder is a favorite subject of stories, songs, even children's nursery rhymes. True-crime books have been popular reading since at least the 1600s, when a book called *God's Revenge Against Murder and Adultery* was a bestseller in England. Victorian readers loved sensational crime coverage, devouring graphic details in popular periodicals like the *Illustrated Police News*.

The horrific crimes of Dr. H. H. Holmes, "America's first serial killer,"

"The fourth and most horrible murder in Whitechapel," 1888. Coverage of the murders carried out by "Jack the Ripper" in London's East End. At least seven women, all but one of whom were prostitutes, were killed and mutilated during a three-month period in 1888. The murderer was never caught. Front page, number 1,283 of the *Illustrated Police News: Law Courts and Weekly Record*. (London, September 15, 1888).

who trapped and murdered possibly hundreds of guests at his Chicago hotel during the 1893 World's Fair (though only a fraction of that number have been confirmed), triggered a media frenzy in the United States that hasn't let up since. As recently as 1991, Jeffrey Dahmer was a *People* magazine cover boy, and tabloids still jockey to coin psychopathic pseudonyms for killer clowns and night stalkers. Peruse your local cable listings and you'll find a host of true-crime programs, exposés, manhunts, and dramatic recreations.

> Lizzy Borden took an ax
> And gave her mother forty whacks
> When she saw what she had done
> She gave her father forty-one.

Black widows, diabolical doctors, cult killers, and Jekyll-and-Hyde Joe-College types grip our culture to a degree that seems obscene, inspiring fan clubs, trading cards, and board games. At the now defunct Museum of Death in Los Angeles, proprietors Cathee Shultz and J. D. Healy not long ago displayed a baseball signed by Charles Manson, paintings of Pogo the Clown by John Wayne Gacy, and other artifacts directly solicited from the jailed killers.

But our widespread fascination with the bloody and monstrous may be healthier than it looks. More than any other unseen "monster," the serial killer represents our deep-seated social fears about random crime, violence, and death. Joking, telling stories, and reading comics about or otherwise bringing the subject into the light where we can see and share it helps calm these fears.
See also: *Horror movies, Murder.*

SHEOL

In ancient Hebrew tradition all dead souls—whether wicked or virtuous—proceed to Sheol. A sort of metaphor for the grave, Sheol has a lot in common with Hades as the ancient Greek poet Homer pictured it. It's a bleak underworld of darkness, dust, and worms where whispering shades lead an ineffectual half-life sans hope or memory.

In the Bible, Job calls Sheol his home and darkness his bed. Even God is forgotten there: "For in death there is no remembrance of thee; in Sheol who will give thee praise?"
See also: *Hereafter.*

SHIVA

After a relative dies, a Jewish family sits shiva, a traditional week of mourning that starts with three days of intense grief followed by four days of eulogy drawn from the Talmud, the set of laws guiding traditional Jewish life. Friends deliver food. The household covers mirrors and keeps candles burning. Men won't shave for the week and may clip their neckties to represent the severing of the dead from the living.

On the seventh day, a rabbi or other representative arrives to "stand up" the mourners, reciting a verse from Isaiah (66:13): "As a mother comforts her child, so shall I the Eternal comfort you . . . and the days of your mourning will come to an end."

For what may be the first time that week, the family ventures outdoors. In a gentle return to the world at large, they walk a slight but vital distance together, perhaps around the block.

SHRINE

A shrine is an altar, chapel, niche, or other place dedicated to and made holy by its association with a certain god, goddess, saint, or other religious icon. But it can also be an impromptu display of artifacts that express personal or collective grief. Spontaneous shrines, such as the nationwide outpouring of candles, flowers, poems, and drawings that appeared in public spaces everywhere in response to the 9/11 attacks in New York City, reflect our need to reach out and express ourselves on the spot. We gathered by the thousands in formerly

September 11, 2001. Photograph by David Finn.

anonymous streets to view these offerings; add our own expressions of horror, grief, and hope; and find temporary relief and comfort in a burden shared.

See also: *Memorial, Monument.*

SHROUD

Perhaps the most famous cloth used to wrap or swaddle a dead body is the Shroud of Turin, which bears a mysterious image of a crucified man. While some call it a clever hoax perpetrated by a skilled medieval artist, others believe it's the very cloth the corpse of Jesus of Nazareth was wrapped and entombed in after the Crucifixion—now a reflection of Christ's passion.

Housed in the Cathedral of Saint John the Baptist in Turin, Italy, the revered fabric has a long history of appearing and disappearing out of the hands of the Catholic Church and has been one of the most studied artifacts in human history, subject to intense scientific scrutiny. Radiocarbon testing of a section of the cloth placed it circa mid-fourteenth century (it would have to be some two thousand years old to qualify as Christ's shroud), but the controversy and the mystery are ongoing.

SIGN OF DEATH

In legend, the sixteenth-century anatomist Andreas Vesalius elicited a grim "Ouch!" while dissecting a presumed-dead body. If this seems far-fetched, consider that as recently as 150 years ago, many medical professionals wouldn't have been able to say for certain whether a patient was dead or alive.

In ancient Greece and Rome, the absence of a heartbeat was the accepted sign of death. The heart was the seat of life, people thought, the first organ to live and the last to die, and the functions of the brain depended on it.

But as it happens, a body can lack a pulse—it can also be cold, senseless, and evidently not breathing—and that still doesn't (necessarily) make it dead.

Throughout much of human history, dying patients weren't formally seen during their last illness or examined by a doctor after they died. It was up to the attending household, to laypeople, to assess the signs and confirm a case. And so, from at least the time of Vesalius on, doctors advised against a hasty funeral. A corpse should remain aboveground for three days before burial, during which time you could administer smelling salts or sneezing powder, stuff tufts of wool up the corpse's nose, hold a mirror to its mouth, or rest a glass on its chest to test for motion of the diaphragm, since the most obvious outward sign of death was—and is—that a person isn't breathing.

"Lend me a looking glass;
If that her breath will mist or stain the stone,
Why then she lives."

—from *King Lear*, by William Shakespeare

For many centuries the absence of a heartbeat and respiration was sufficient to pronounce someone dead, but today's doctors prefer to make the call when all parts of the brain, especially the brain stem, have stopped working. Starved of oxygen, brain cells instantly begin to expire, and when enough do, the body reaches a point of no return. Historically the term "brain death" meant a determination of death when no activity is detected in the brain. Today, brain-death criteria are medically and legally used to pronounce a person dead even if life-support equipment keeps the body's metabolic processes working.

See also: *Burial—premature, Security coffins, Waiting mortuaries.*

SIN EATING

In the early days of Christianity, sinners were obliged to repent in public. You might, for instance, be expected to right a moral wrong by standing outside the church door day and night, rain or shine, all through Lent.

In the Middle Ages, private prayer and charitable deeds replaced the tradition of public penance, but the Catholic view held that a kind of residue remained on the soul even after penance and confession; sinners who bore these traces when they died had to endure the agonies of a good cleansing in purgatory before proceeding on to the kingdom of heaven.

Select deeds—fighting in a crusade against the Saracens, embarking on a pilgrimage, building a church, giving to the poor—as determined by the Church could scrub away those traces (on behalf of your own soul or that of a departed loved one) with a partial "indulgence." Some works even wiped the slate clean, so to speak, earning a full indulgence.

By the thirteenth century, people were "buying" forgiveness this way, and the Church grew increasingly dependent on the earnings. In 1517, Martin Luther made this trafficking in "indulgences" central to his Reformation movement, calling it a glaring example of Roman corruption.

Another way of easing the soul's burden of sin was through the practice of sin eating. To consume food that had been situated over the dead person's heart was to relieve his or her spirit from the weight of sin. Many English villages had their own semi-official sin eaters, and sometimes the poor were hired for the occasion (we can only hope someone paid the service forward later on!).

Usually the practice took place at the end of a wake, when all the mourners were gathered for the procession. The corpse was brought out of the house, and as a contemporary in Herefordshire described it: "laid on a bier; a loaf of bread was brought out, and delivered to the sin eater over the corpse, as also a mazer bowl full of beer, which he was to drink up, and six pence in money, in consideration whereof he took upon him all the sins of the defunct, and freed him from walking after he was dead."

In North Wales, a bowl full of milk was provided instead of beer. A related custom was to give the mourners cake, cheese, beer, and milk across the coffin in exchange for money offerings that were placed on a board by the altar.

Dutch settlers in the New World baked burial cakes and marked them with the initials of the deceased, to be eaten by mourners at the funeral, a custom adapted from the earlier tradition of formal sin eating.

See also: *Food*.

SOUL

The soul is usually held to be our true or spiritual self, the essential or animating part of us that many cultures believe survives death.

Most traditional peoples think of the body and soul as distinct and believe that after death the two split off and continue on to separate destinations: the body goes back to its origins while the soul is "liberated" to wander free, merge with ancestors, cross vast waters, or head up or down to heaven or hell.

In creation stories from around the world, body and soul begin as different substances. In the Bible, God formed the first man's body out of clay, but Adam didn't live until God breathed into his nostrils. Variations of this story occur all over world, even among remote tribes with no access to Hebrew doctrine. Arc-

tic Eurasians believe the soul and body are made by different gods, the body most often of clay and the soul of snow or a god's breath. Pundjel, the Australian aboriginal creator god, modeled humans of clay before lying down on them and breathing into their mouths, nostrils, and navels. Maoris of New Zealand have Tiki, who kneaded red clay with his own sweat to form a ball, into which he breathed life.

Not only is the soul widely believed to be separate from the body, it tends to have its own distinct elements. The divided or dual soul is an almost universal motif, though the two or more aspects are often confused.

In Egyptian cosmology, the term stands for a whole host of energies. Scholars disagree as to how many and how these fragments of the soul behave after death, but there are anywhere from between four and eight, the most familiar of which are the *ka*, or vital force—the body double of a person that functions like a guardian spirit after death—and the *ba*, which most resembles the Western idea of the soul as self-consciousness, memory, and perception. The *ba* is most often depicted as a bird with a human head and shows the soul as it appears on earth after a person has died.

Aristotle acknowledged three parts of the soul with different functions: the vegetative soul maintained bodily vitality, the animative soul regulated motion and sensation, and the rational soul governed the higher life of the mind. The rational soul could die without affecting the body; animals managed an entire lifetime without one. But the death of the vegetative soul always resulted in bodily death.

In a number of traditions the soul is a dual entity, with the higher soul or life essence aligned with breath, wind, fire, light, heat, a spark, a star, and the heart. The Romans called this higher spirit the animus (breath or wind). Immaterial and formless, it's the basis of our moral, spiritual, and intellectual self and is rarely conceived of as an image of the body. When the body dies, the higher soul flees to be with gods or ancestors in a next or blessed world, while the lower "shadow" soul or "body" soul hangs on, coveting and identifying with the body.

The lower soul is more animal, associated with passion, desire, darkness, blood, bone, earth, shadow, and danger. It is widely thought of as a body double (the German word for ghost, *doppelgänger,* means "double-goer"), though it can also shape-shift, become animal or bird, fly, and appear in dreams. The lower soul is intensely connected to the physical body and has a hard time severing its bond in the physical plane. It may, like a shadow or reflection, hang around the corpse, and so haunt or harm the living. This lower shadowlike soul is most likely to linger on after death, wreaking havoc. When the higher and lower souls separate, the lower is left without insight or conscience. Childlike and inclined to anger, robbed of its higher nature, the lower soul remains attached to a useless body, bound to the deceased's unrestrained passions, to longing, and must be appeased and respectfully eased out of the picture lest it slip back into the body and carry on in the form of the undead or become an angry ghost. Only complete decomposition of the body destroys or frees the lower soul.

In modern Greece, the time between burial and ritual safety is forty days. In other cultures every bit of flesh must be off the bones. Jewish custom calls for several years, after which family may disinter and gather up the purified bones and lay them to rest in a family sepulchre. Zoroastrians and Tibetans accelerate things by exposing the corpse to predators and the elements, while Hindus cremate the body. Each culture has definite rites for easing the peril of a fresh corpse and helping the lower soul on its way.

In 1907, to deduce the weight of a human soul, Dr. Duncan MacDougall fashioned a unique bed scale. He positioned his dying patients on it, and at the instant of their demise, sought a downward twitch of the needle. The human soul, he deduced after weighing many subjects, weighs three-quarters of an ounce—roughly the same as the big toe. See also: *Appeasing the dead, Funerary rites, Ghosts, Hauntings, Hereafter, Undead.*

SPIRIT PHOTOGRAPHY

In 1861 a Boston jewelry engraver and amateur photographer named William Mumler took an experimental self-

techniques like double exposure or exposing the same frame of film twice; shooting with long exposures, which creates blur; sandwiching negatives together in the enlarger; or today by digitally manipulating the image. It's hard to fathom how pictures like this ever duped anyone; but photographic science was still largely mysterious to the average person at the time, and a "willing" public had little cause not to believe their own eyes.

Though never the most credible aspect of the spiritualist movement, spirit photography remained popular well into the twentieth century.
See also: *Postmortem photography, Spiritualism.*

portrait and developed the plate, startled to find what appeared to be a spectral female face hovering by his own. Careful inspection showed that he had double-exposed the image, but with spiritualism at its peak, Mumler fast saw the value of this novel trick.

Working as a fraudulent medium, he photographed his sitters—for a considerable fee—adding in ghostly likenesses of dead relatives or celebrities at the developing stage.

His new pastime caught the fancy of an eager public and helped fuel the international spread of spiritualism. Though Mumler was caught in the act rather early in the game, he had many imitators, including, in the 1920s, William Hope and his famous Crewe Circle; Hope perfected the technique of adding "extras" to unexposed film and had an extensive following.

Spirit photography can be created in-camera or in the darkroom using basic

SPIRITUALISM

The idea that the human spirit lives on after death and that the living might communicate with the dead through an intermediary is nothing new. But the formal religious movement known as spiritualism got its start in 1848 with two bored teenage girls.

When the Fox sisters began communicating with a resident spirit in their ordinary farmhouse in western New York, teaching the ghost to rap in code on the walls, the United States was in the thick of territorial and economic growth. This was a progressive age, when Samuel Morse's telegraph offered an expansive vision for the future. To those just encountering his mysterious electrical force, the idea of a similar system linking the living and the dead, a sort of "spirit telegram," must have seemed a real and tangible possibility.

Spiritualism was especially attractive to women, who still very much dominated in the domestic realm. In mid-nineteenth-century New York State, some half of deaths were of children under five. What grieving mother wouldn't take comfort in the idea of contacting her lost one in another plane, of "lifting the veil" to reach across to the other side? To the spiritualists, death wasn't an end but a transformation. They wore white at funerals, where mediums intercepted messages from the souls newly settled in heaven ("Summerland" in spiritualist parlance).

Suddenly everyone was hosting séances and Spirit Circles, where men and women held hands to attract spirit with shared energy. Invitations for "tea and table tilting" (a form of spirit communication wherein a small parlor table tipped, tilted, rapped, or vibrated in response to sitters' questions) or to consult a Ouija board were commonplace.

Many spiritualists turned to the teachings of Emanuel Swedenborg, an influential Swedish philosopher and mystic who claimed to have seen the spirit world in trancelike visions, recording what he observed there in *Heaven and Hell* and other theological works.

Within a few years, tens of thousands of Americans and Europeans were flocking to séances, and the spiritualist movement had engaged everyone from politicians to poets, including Sir Arthur Conan Doyle, author of the Sherlock Holmes books. Though still practiced today, spiritualism as a popular movement waned in the early twentieth century as skeptics like Harry Houdini hastened to discredit it and exposed the techniques of fraudulent mediums.
See also: *Fox sisters, Houdini, Lily Dale, Medium, Spirit photography.*

STOPPING CLOCKS

Death stops time. The metaphor is powerful, and in lore, spirits are not always conscious that death has claimed them, that time is no longer their concern.

To shelter the living and speed the dead on their way, it became customary to stop ticking clocks (and later watches, too, by extension) whenever a death occurred; the new silence helped signal to a spirit that it was time to go, that it needn't remain in or near the body.

Because clocks and watches were purposely stopped as close to the instant of death as possible, the related idea arose that death stopped clocks; the final tick of a treasured timepiece was a signal for the Angel of Death to claim the owner's soul. See also: *Funerary rites, Wake.*

SUICIDE

According to the World Health Organization, which designated September 10 World Suicide Prevention Day in 2006, more people die annually of their own accord—some 1 million worldwide—than as a result of war and homicide combined. In the last forty-five years, suicide rates have increased by 60 percent worldwide, with suicide now among the three leading causes of death among people between the ages of fifteen and forty-four years.

Historical attitudes about suicide vary. In many traditions, the act is viewed as a spiritual or actual crime. It insults the fates, spites the creator, or usurps the natural order, damaging the soul in the process.

Hindu faith holds that people who die by their own hand face heavy karma for many lifetimes, until the balance is restored. In Britain, suicide and attempted suicide were illegal until 1961, and in many parts of Europe, they still are—at least on the books.

Both the ancient Greeks and Romans believed that a good death was as important as a good life, making suicide supportable in certain circumstances. The Greek philosopher Socrates killed himself in 399 BC, after being convicted of heresy in Athens, by drinking a cup of poison hemlock.

"If a body is useless," asked Seneca, a first-century Roman philosopher and statesman, "why should one not free the struggling soul?"

But Christianity introduced the idea of suicide as self-murder, calling it a moral sin opposed to the sanctity of life. The bodies of Christians who died by their own hands were buried in unconsecrated ground; their souls, it was understood, proceeded to hell.

The Vatican's 1980 Declaration on Euthanasia pronounced that "intentionally causing one's own death, or suicide, is . . . equally as wrong as murder, such an action . . . is to be considered as a rejection of God's sovereignty and loving plan."

Whether mercy killing or act of despair, suicide has always inspired controversy. The nineteenth-century German philosopher Friedrich Nietzsche called it "a great source of comfort," a kind of insurance against suffering that allowed him "a calm passage . . . across many a dark night."

A 2006 *Discover* magazine article cites a study wherein poets who committed suicide were compared with those of similar backgrounds who died naturally. Using text-analysis software, researchers at the University of Pennsylvania and the University of Texas at Austin had compared 156 poems by nine poets who committed suicide to 135 poems written by nine poets who didn't. Suicides like Sylvia Plath, they found, favored first-person singular references like "I," "me," and "my" in their poetry. The other camp tended toward plural terms like "we," "us," and "our." Suicidal poets were also inclined to neglect communication words like "talk," "share," and "listen" in their work. The moral seems to be, Talk to someone first, even if you feel like you have no one in your life you *can* talk to.

In 1953 a vicar named Chad Varah founded the Samaritans organization in London to give people who feel alone in a time of despair a confidential and impartial place to turn to twenty-four hours a day, and the Samaritans still offer these same services today. Many thousands of trained volunteers have responded to millions of distress calls over the years, as many as 4.6 million in a single year.

See also: *Euthanasia.*

SUPERSTITION

Whether or not we think of ourselves as superstitious, we're surrounded by ideas and images that have resonated in our collective unconscious since the human race began.

Whether they relate to the dead body itself or fuel omens about death, superstitions on the theme are always colorful. Consider, for instance, the seventeenth-century idea that the corpse of a murder victim will bleed profusely when its killer walks into the room or that corpses cut new teeth and continue to grow hair and fingernails after death.

And omens of death abound: if a rooster crowed at midnight, if two black crows convened on a laundry line, if crickets suddenly fled your house, if you washed your clothes on Good Friday or unwittingly sat thirteen at a table, if a picture fell off the wall or flowers bloomed out of season, if a robin perched on one of your chairs or you strayed within a dead man's sight or you heard the *tap-tap-tick* of the wood-bearing "death watch" beetle in your walls . . . someone near at hand was a goner.

And this in the British Isles alone!

To glimpse someone's fetch or *doppelgänger* bespoke an accident, drowning, or other tragedy. Most frightening of all was to encounter your own double, though some believed that if you spotted yourself in the lane at daybreak, you could expect a long life. Later in the day, you were done for.

More often heard than seen, the banshee—*bean sidhe* or "fairy woman"—made her wailing racket whenever a death was imminent, especially a death in a noble Irish family. If she did manifest and you managed to steal a look at her, she was as likely as not combing her long white hair while she wailed.

In Scotland's Orkney Islands, people believed that each human being had a spirit, or *varden,* that accompanied her or him through life, usually in the form of an animal. When death was near, the *varden* showed itself and howled dismally.

Dogs howling in the dark of night are never a good sign, but especially dread-inspiring are the shaggy, calf-size black dogs or black hounds, supernatural beasts with enormous glowing red eyes. Most often encountered on lonely tracks, ancient roads, crossroads, bridges, and other places of human transition, they've also, paradoxically, been known to guide lost travelers home. Sir Arthur Conan Doyle's *Sherlock Holmes* classic, *The Hound of the Baskervilles,* draws on this regional tradition. Hundreds of black dog sightings have been recorded in England, Scotland, and Brittany over the past four hundred years, as well as in Denmark and other parts of Scandinavia.

Many in Madagascar dread *Dauben-tonia madagascariensis,* or the aye-aye, deeming it a harbinger of death (should it turn its long, crooked finger your way, you'll be the next to die). Luckily not all Malagasy feel this way; some islanders revere the peculiar-looking primate.

See also: *Bees and hives, Birds, Ghosts, Halloween, Undead.*

When will I die? is a question that lives under our skin, and for better or worse we like to play at fore-telling or divining the answer. The "death" card in traditional tarot packs is often wrongly read or inter-preted literally (it more accurately stands for the pains of change).

On Saint Mark's Eve in North Oxfordshire, England, young peo-ple used to gather in the church-yard as the clock struck 11:00 p.m. and hold still and silent until it struck 1:00, awaiting a procession of all the people who would die in the coming year.

Today a number of online death "clocks" will calculate the precise moment of a person's demise.

SYMBOLS

Many of the familiar symbols we see carved on tombs and gravestones and tend to take for granted have quite specific meanings. Others are less familiar. The ancient Greeks, for instance, believed the soul left the body in the form of a butterfly, so the insect became a symbol of death and resurrection. (The butterfly was also later thought to carry the souls of children who had died before baptism.)

During the plague years in medieval Europe—with the populace understandably consumed by the concept of inevitable or untimely death—the skeleton or skull emerged as a familiar symbol. The broken or draped column, the weeping willow, the hourglass weighted with sand, and the scythe, representing a life cut short, are other established symbols of loss and mourning.

A Jewish gravestone might show the Star of David or a menorah, while Christian graves often featured angels, referencing an afterlife in heaven; doves, the Holy Spirit and peace; a lily, evoking the Virgin Mother and purity; or a lamb, likewise a sign of purity and innocence, most often attributed to a child.

See also: *Birds.*

TAXIDERMY

The word comes from the ancient Greek words *taxis,* meaning movement, and *derma,* meaning skin, but taxidermists—whether hunter-hobbyists or professional staffers at a natural history museum—do more than move or arrange skin. They need skill in tanning, molding, casting,

carpentry, and woodworking as well as a knowledge of anatomy, dissection, sculpture, painting, and drawing.

To make a lifelike three-dimensional representation of an animal for display, the skin—including fur, feathers, or scales—is removed, preserved, and replaced or mounted over an artificial armature to appear lifelike. Manmade materials may be used in place of natural ones.

Crypto-taxidermy means creating stuffed animals that have no living counterpart—the mythical or extinct, such as unicorns and jackalopes.

TEETH

Hardest of human bones, teeth are a key component of modern archeology. Even after bones and skulls have rotted and turned to dust, teeth can last thousands of years. The ancient Egyptians were already extracting them, often fetching teeth back from the dentist to be buried with a body so the deceased would make it to the afterlife with a full set. In medieval times, when bones and other relics of the dead were vital to medicine and magic, teeth from a dead man's skull were especially valued. Tie up a few in a bag together with the foot of a mole, hang it by the chimney, and you could guard your entire family against toothaches. This sort of "preventive dentistry" was eventually replaced by innovative new ways of exploiting these hardest of human bones. Since false teeth carved from ivory or other substances rarely held up when set in living jaws, the nineteenth-century American dentist Levi S. Parmly figured out how to get hold of really hard replacement teeth. He and his brother combed the site of the 1814 Battle of Bridgewater for days, at the end of which Parmly gleefully reported a harvest of "thousands of teeth, extracted from bodies, of all ages, that have fallen in battle." These relics of war ended up in other people's dentures, which Parmly rightly claimed would "last a lifetime."

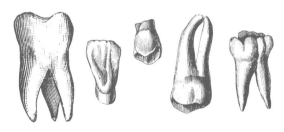

In a ritual occurring no later than puberty, Balinese go to temple for the filing of the teeth. The six upper front teeth are ground until utterly even. Ignore this obligation in life, and your soul might meet the gods with jagged fangs, be mistaken for a demon, and end up barred from the spirit world.

THANATOLOGY
The study of all things relating to death, dying, and grief.

TOMB
A tomb, or structure in which a corpse is buried, might be aboveground or completely or partially below it. The Egyptian pyramids are royal tombs, as is the Taj Mahal, built by the Indian emperor Shah Jahan for his wife in the seventeenth century. Conceived of as the most magnificent memorial on earth, it was a symbol of the emperor's great love. His own tomb across the river was never finished, so he is buried beside her.
See also: *Catacomb, Charnel house, Crypt Memorial, Sarcophogus.*

UNDEAD

Many cultures fear retribution from reanimated corpses.

Individuals who died suddenly or violently—murder and plague victims, suicides, battlefield casualties, unbaptized infants—had a special inclination to "walk" after death and wreak havoc, as did criminals or people who were improperly buried. Witches and sorcerers might resurrect a body through necromantic means, to carry out some errand.

Today, vampires and zombies are our most familiar "undead," and the figures in best-selling books and Hollywood movies have ancient precedents in myth, folklore, and religion.

The word "vampire" comes from the Slavic *upir,* but creatures of this description are also acknowledged in India, Africa, China, the Philippines, Central America, and South America.

Vampires in rural folklore little resemble the love interests or protagonists in novels by Stephenie Meyer or Anne Rice, which in turn draw on the gothic model established by Bram Stoker in his 1897 book *Dracula.* Stoker based his archetypal bloodsucker on Vlad Tepes, a thirteenth-century Transylvanian nobleman nicknamed "Dracul" or "Dracula," meaning "devil" or "dragon," and "Vlad the Impaler," for his favorite method of dispatching enemies.

But your average village vampire was neither aristocratic nor romantic. He was a swarthy peasant type—ugly, squat, and bloated—a greedy, wretched loner opposed to life, order, fertility, and productivity. Vampires brought drought and foul weather. They drained the life from crops, the milk from animals, and the blood from humans. They carried out their mischief and may-

hem between midnight and dawn, and sometimes in dreams. Some were merely sullen and restless—as likely to throw rocks through windows as to suck your blood—while others ate fellow corpses and spread filth and pestilence. Many shifted form, appearing as wolves, horses, donkeys, goats, cats, owls, mice, and frogs, and might, with a glance, render a person unconscious or insane.

In short, vampires were blamed for any and all misfortune.

If mourners had persistent visions of someone newly deceased or any of the above ensued, villagers disinterred and examined a body in question. Telltale signs were a cracked or sunken grave mound; a body that had failed to discolor or decay; a face sporting red cheeks; flexible, bloated limbs; new fingernails or skin growing under the old; a white liver; or an open or bloody mouth.

To fend off a vampire, you needed cow dung found under a hawthorn bush, garlic, or green nutshells. You could smear the sign of the cross on your front door with tar, create a barrier of water between you and the creature, or in Pomerania (present-day Poland), dip part of a shroud in the vampire's blood, steep the blood in brandy, and drink the elixir down. This made you resistant to *all* vampires (an interesting contrast to the familiar idea that vampire blood spreads vampirism and must be avoided).

In the Balkans, a vampire is obliged to keep to its grave on Saturdays, so this is the safest day to seek and destroy it with a stake through the heart (some vampires have two, so mind you, get the *right* heart). In Serbia, vampire hunters snip the knee ligaments of the corpse to prevent it from walking again. The head can also be removed and reburied, provided enough earth is layered between to prevent the vampire from reaching its head. Fire, and cremation, of course, are a lethal last resort.

Hollywood zombies are slow-moving heaps of murderous rot, usually entranced by a master with evil intent. But the zombie tradition, a component of Haitian voodoo ritual influenced by a West African python cult, holds that a dead person can be revived by a *bokor,* or voodoo sorcerer, who then controls the zombie, which has no will of its own. "Zombi" is another name of the voodoo snake god Damballah Wedo. The serpent, which sheds its skin and emerges renewed, works well as a symbol of reanimation, but researchers like Wade Davis, author of *The Serpent and the Rainbow,* claim a zombie isn't a reanimated corpse at all: it's a person freed from the thralls of inhibitory toxic drugs.

Davis proposed that when precisely administered by a skilled voodoo practitioner, a powder containing tetrodoxin—a powerful poison associated with the puffer fish—will evoke a paralytic state known as thanatomimesis, which mimics death. After this and a second secret powder are administered, the "zombie" may then be handled like a corpse, provided with a funeral service, and buried. The numbed victim is later removed from the grave and restored to "life" through a series of prescribed rituals and maintained as a kind of semihuman automaton.

See also: *Necromancy, Superstition.*

UNDERTAKER

Also known as a funeral director or mortician, an undertaker oversees funerals, prepares bodies for burial or cremation, and may also be an embalmer.

URN

A vase or container used to hold the cremated remains ("cremains") of the dead, an urn can vary in size and shape and is sometimes set on a pedestal. Funerary urns were and are used by a great many civilizations and cultures. The ancient Romans placed them in niches, in group tombs called *columbariums.*

See also: *Cremation, Memorials.*

VALHALLA

Old Norse heroes crossed the Rainbow Bridge to Asgard, realm of the gods, and spent eternity in Valhalla, a splendid Hall of the Slain. In Norse mythology, dead warriors are welcomed to the hall by none other than Odin, the "All-father of the gods" himself. Here they'll live until the Ragnarok (Doomsday), when they'll march through the doors for the last time to fight at Odin's side against the giants.

Meanwhile, they enjoy Odin and his fellow deities as companions, play warrior games by day, and convene at night to feast on pork and mead. Since entry depends on a valorous death rather than a virtuous life, and since all warriors were male, only men resided in Valhalla—though they're waited on by supernatural female beings called Valkyries.

Originally demons that feasted on the spoils of war, Valkyries haunted battlefields, swooping among the dead on massive, glossy wings. Because of their black feathers, the Valkyries were also called *kraken,* or ravens. Warriors who fell in battle and whose corpses were not claimed by fellows were termed *hrafengrennir,* "raven feeders."

When the idea of Valhalla evolved from a battlefield to a paradise for warriors, the Valkyries morphed too, into beneficent female superheroes. When they weren't pouring mead in Valhalla, these winged female beings served Odin, helping to guide the course of human battles and leading fallen warriors to their reward in Asgard.

WAILING AND LAMENTATION

In Jewish tradition, the day or so between death and burial is the "wailing time," or *aninut,* from a Hebrew word meaning "to wail, complain, or lament."

Wailing in the face of death is no longer standard practice in Western culture and is more likely discouraged today as excessive. But in the past, holding back would have seemed strange.

In ancient Greece, women encircled a body, holding the deceased's head or tearing their own hair while belting out a mournful lament. Relatives might keep to one side of the body while professional "keeners" stood stationed on the other. Together they wove the wailing back and forth, binding orderly traditional chants together with more intimate improvisations. In Greece, Portugal, and other countries, people still hold great respect for professional keeners, women (very few cultures have male lamenters) hired to share and help shape their family's grief into a harmonious goodbye.

Women also wail and chant at Akan funerals in Ghana—an important job, since in this as in many other traditions, a lament is a measure of the deceased's worth, so the bolder the better. What's more, they enter trances to possess the dead person's spirit: talking, walking, and dancing as the departed did, relaying his words and wishes.

Even in the distant past, many frowned on demonstrative mourning, calling it rude and disruptive. Early Christians discouraged it outright: wild lamentation flew in the face of afterlife doctrine, since to leave this life of toil was to earn a far improved version in heaven. Why fuss? Death must be viewed as a joyful release. But for many, the need to express basic human love and loss overruled such edicts.

See also: *Funerary rites, Mourning.*

WAITING MORTUARIES

In nineteenth-century Europe, medical uncertainty about the signs of death, and rumors and reports of premature burial, had the public in a state of near panic. A young French physician named Jean-Jacques Bruhier suggested a system of morgues, or receiving houses, where the dead could be watched for up to seventy-two hours or until they began to putrefy. Bruhier's ideas for reforming burial practices circled Europe, and waiting mortuaries sprang up in major cities, especially in Germany.

One system in Berlin attached the fingers of each corpse to a huge bell with strings. If the hand stirred, presumably the bell would sound. Another offered separate rooms for male and female cadavers. A third in Munich offered "luxury" chambers alongside the "common," and theoretically the once-and-future corpse announced itself via a giant harmonium with air-pressured bellows to which its fingers and toes were tied or otherwise attached. For a fee, tourists could amble through this place and take in the pretty statues and floral displays and, of course, the major attraction: putrefying corpses. One particularly cutting-edge waiting mortuary in Vienna, circa 1860, stationed attendants by an extensive panel of electric bells corresponding to the corpse-inhabited beds in the ward.

In Germany, the expensive—and undignified, many contemporaries argued—waiting mortuaries hung on for more than a hundred years, though no residents actually sat up and breathed anew. See also: *Burial—premature, Coffin—security, Sign of death, Wake.*

WAKE

In many traditions, close watch must be kept over a corpse until it is buried. A dead body must never be left alone. In some cultures, people "watch" for a living: the more paid watchers a family hires and the longer their vigil, the more honor and status is due that family's name.

The death vigil ensures that a body really is dead while keeping away predators, scavengers, and evil spirits as necessary. What's more, the fretful spirit takes comfort and consolation in the company before its journey.

Certainly a wake is a chance for survivors to console one another, though certain customs and prohibitions must be observed: candles are kept burning at all times, for instance, and must be lit one from another; the ashes from the fire shouldn't be removed until the coffin has exited; all pictures and mirrors must be covered.

Irish Catholics have a particularly rich tradition. In *The Mourner's Dance,* Katherine Ashenburg describes what was until relatively recently the typical Irish Catholic or "merry" wake in Newfoundland. Such wakes might last all night or longer. Usually visitors greeted the family with a proper Irish "sorry for your trouble" before approaching the coffin. To kiss or touch the corpse's forehead was to ensure the person wouldn't return in your dreams; praise was another fond precaution.

Visitors roved back and forth between the wake room and the social center of the house, the kitchen, where neighbors

An Irish wake, from a sketch by M. Woolf. *Harper's Weekly*, v. 17, March 15, 1873.

had ham, shorebirds, baked beans, fish cakes, rolls, pancakes, sweets, and plenty of drink. At least three lunches or "scoffs" were served that night, with distributions of bread, cheese, and whisky at midnight.

Around then, immediate family usually retired for the evening, and the "time," as Newfoundlanders call a social gathering, really got under way. People recited ghost stories and playful rhymes about the deceased. There were pantomimes, bawdy songs, and pranks like stringing fishing line here and there to make the corpse's head bob, a hand wave, or the torso rise in its coffin. A dead hand was at least as likely as one living to end up holding an ice cream cone or an ace of spades. If the body in question was elderly—a young person's wake was duly solemn —games might feature the penalty of

kissing the corpse or biting its toes.

The idea of a boisterous party at a time like this might offend some people today, but folklorists argue that "merry" wakes satisfy an ancient belief in the spiteful spirit.

If in fact the dead envy the living, what better way to bridge that unprotected span of time between death and burial— when a restless soul is snagged between worlds—than to make like they're still alive? Deal the dead into a game of cards. Make them the life of the party. Rowdy drinking, ridicule, and shenanigans were all forms of subversive license taken to shield survivors. They also, of course, offered emotional relief and release by asserting "the vitality of the living," says Ashenburg. "People are uncomfortable with the thought," she points out, "but death can make those left behind feel piercingly, singularly alive in a way that nothing else can.

Caterers will tell you that people eat much more at a funeral than a wedding. Jokes at a wake or after a funeral can seem disproportionately funny."

See also: *Appeasing the dead, Burial—premature, Coffins—safety, Waiting mortuaries.*

WAR

In humanity's distant hunter-gatherer past, spears, slings and arrows, flint ax heads, and daggers were all dreamed up and used to kill and prepare game. But people soon deduced what else these deadly tools could do and engaged in warfare, a pastime we humans share with only a handful of other species.

Archeological evidence—including the fabled "walls," a stone tower, and other fortifications—hints that as far back as the biblical city of Jericho, one of the oldest human settlements on earth, people engaged their clubs and spears in battle.

The early Bronze Age brought the mace, a stone the size of a small bowling ball mounted on a handle that made for effortless bashing. This new weapon was strictly military—no point pummeling your dinner—and inspired other innovations. Implements of death were eventually crafted of copper, bronze, and iron, and swords, slings, catapults, and armor would one day give way to modern weaponry: rifles, Panzer tanks, and atom bombs among them.

In the twentieth century alone, more than 200 million people were

killed in wars. Between 1914 and 1918, 61,526,000 soldiers were mobilized for World War I, and within four years, 8.3 million of them were dead. Civilian casualties would reach 8 million.

Twenty-one years later, more or less the same players staged another world war just like the first, with an even greater toll in human lives. World War II also debuted a horrifying new weapon: in 1941, the United States loosed an atom bomb on Hiroshima, wiping out 66,000 people instantly. Three days later, another bomb hit Nagasaki, killing 39,000 more.

The ongoing U.S. war in Iraq has, at the time of this writing, claimed more than 4,000 U.S. and coalition casualties.

✦ ✦ ✦

WATER

Water is often associated with death, purity, and cleansing.

Hindus believe the Ganges in India is a holy river. To die by it is to be spared rebirths and to unite sooner with Brahman. If a person is too sick or distant to travel to the river in time, family and friends may bring the river instead, spooning mouthfuls into dying mouths.

In folklore, water—which assumes any shape but holds none and which, like a mirror, reflects—can irresistibly attract or even absorb dead souls. The soul, itself a reflection (of the body, which is why ghosts often appear as the physical body did in life), is "captured" by being reflected in water. So water may also be used as a barrier to keep the newly dead from turning back toward the corpse or wandering home. In many funeral ceremonies, especially Hindu rites, water is poured across the path when mourners leave a gravesite, and the idea that the dead can't or won't cross water inspired some societies to literally remove "dangerous" dead (criminals, murder victims, and others likely to "walk" after death) to islands to enclose them.

Among Celts, Scandinavians, Greeks, and other maritime cultures, the realm of the dead was portrayed as an island. Usually the deceased was ferried there by boat, never to return. There are a number of rivers in the Greek underworld, besides the Styx, over which Charon ferried the dead for a fee (often a coin left under the tongue of the corpse), including a river of woe, a river of wailing, and Lethe, the river of forgetfulness, from which all new arrivals must drink. Africans living near what used to be called the Guinea Coast believed the souls of the dead could only earn eternal peace once they had crossed three rivers and climbed a mountain. Some African-American spirituals refer to "crossing over Jordan."

With death so often a journey over water, many societies buried real or model ships with their dead to assure their passage.

In crowded Venice, for logistical reasons, gondolas literally carry the body and the mourning procession over water, crossing to the cemetery island of San Michele.

See also: *Funerary rites, Mirrors, Soul.*

WIDOW SACRIFICE

The Egyptians and other ancient and traditional cultures around the world—from Africa and New Zealand to North America and the Fiji Islands—engaged in the practice of widow sacrifice.

In late imperial China, widows who remarried were considered impure, while splendid gateways were constructed in a widow's honor if she committed suicide. Viking wives or unmarried women were often added to the cremation pyre. Way back in the fourth century BC, Alexander the Great's soldiers were the first westerners to note the Hindu custom of sati (or suttee)—where a widow throws herself on her husband's funeral pyre. As one Hindu text puts it: "If her husband is happy, [a wife] should be happy, if he is sad she should be sad, and if he is dead she should also die." No parallel exists for a widower, and though sati was banned in 1929, sporadic cases are still reported in India.

See also: *Murder, Suicide.*

WILL

(OR *LAST WILL AND TESTAMENT*)

For the ancient Romans, a will was a simple legal document that divvied up goods and property, though it might also include burial instructions, provisions for family, and charitable bequests. Women and the poor didn't bother: a woman's wealth and property were her husband's, and the poor owned too little to justify the exercise. Many wills were penned on deathbeds or dictated to lawyers, clergymen, or professional scriveners before witnesses.

In the twelfth century, the will morphed into a religious document and was viewed as a sacred duty, with the Church enforcing its preparation under pain of excommunication. All but the most destitute had to prepare one or risk having their bodies banned from the churchyard or cemetery.

Until the 1700s, a will had two important sections. First, a declaration of faith and piety beginning with a line like "I commend my soul to my creator." This part redressed wrongs and pled forgiveness for injuries inflicted on others. Then on to practical matters: "He wishes and desires that his debts be paid and made good by his executor," that this and that be done in terms of candles, a funeral procession and burial, and epitaphs or memorial plaques. Last but not least, this second section saw to the distribution of a person's inheritance and to charitable endowments (alms). A man of means by the time of his death in 1616, the playwright William Shakespeare willed his wife, Anne Hathaway, his "second-best bed." To today's ears, this sounds like yet another example of the Bard's famous wit; in fact, it was common practice for a man to will his best items to his children and the second best to his wife.

Today a will is more or less what it became again in the eighteenth century, a legal document asserting the right and duty to arrange for one's wealth and property (though many do include funeral and burial instructions, along with more intimate thoughts on how the person would like to be mourned).

During the fourteenth and fifteenth centuries, the will also acted as a kind of literary genre with pros and amateurs alike waxing poetic on the parchment, recording their musings on the inevitability of death and the sweet fleetings of life. Though composed much later—in the nineteenth century—and not as part of her will per se, Christina Rossetti's poem "Song" eloquently fulfills one nonobligatory aspect of a will's function: to teach those left behind how to mourn.

> When I am dead, my dearest,
> Sing no sad songs for me;
> Plant thou no roses at my head,
> Nor shady cypress tree:
> Be the green grass above me
> With showers and dewdrops wet;
> And if thou wilt, remember,
> And if thou wilt, forget.
> —Christina Rossetti, from "Song"

WILL–LIVING

This document takes effect before death, letting doctors and caregivers know what to do when patients become too ill or incapacitated to decide their own fate. The living will lets a person dictate when or whether life-sustaining treatments such as cardiopulmonary resuscitation, artificial respiration, nutrition, and hydration, or the use of antibiotics or painkillers, should be brought to bear or discontinued.

WREATHS

The biblical story of Noah and the flood hints at how old the symbolic use of greenery is. The Egyptians cultivated special gardens to support their custom of making crowns for the dead—a living sacrifice of sorts, a bright offering to keep the spirit present and content in the world beyond, where it wouldn't plague the living. Our use of wreaths probably also owes something to the Greek and Roman practice of using laurel wreaths to crown military victors, star athletes, and kings and emperors.

Every small child who has watched Disney's movie *The Lion King* is familiar with the term "the circle of life," and the shape of a funeral wreath evokes many symbols of the cycle of life and death—from the sun to Samsara, the endless wheel of existence in Buddhist teaching.

The original goal of placing a funeral wreath on a grave or a door may have been to trap, appease, or waylay the dead by offering a live distraction; but today a wreath is just one of the many heartfelt and unassuming ways we say goodbye.

SELECTED BIBLIOGRAPHY

Aries, Philippe. *The Hour of Our Death* (New York: Viking, 1982).

Armstrong, Karen. *A History of God* (New York: Knopf, 1994).

Ashenburg, Katherine. *Mourner's Dance: What We Do When People Die* (New York: North Point Press, 2002).

Ashton, John, and Tom Whyte. *The Quest for Paradise: Visions of Heaven and Eternity in the World's Myths and Religions* (San Francisco: HarperCollins, 2001).

*Barnard, Bryn. *Outbreak: Plagues That Changed History* (New York: Crown, 2005).

*Blackwood, Gary L. *Long-Ago Lives* (New York: Benchmark Books, 2000).

Blum, Deborah. *Ghost Hunters: William James and the Search for Scientific Proof of Life After Death* (New York: Penguin, 2006).

Bondeson, Jan. *Buried Alive: The Terrifying History of Our Most Primal Fear* (New York: Norton, 2001).

Brennan, Herbie. *Death: The Great Mystery of Life* (New York: Carroll & Graf, 2002).

Cantor, Norman. *The Encyclopedia of the Middle Ages* (New York: Viking, 1999).

Carmichael, Elizabeth, and Chloe Sayer. *The Skeleton at the Feast: The Day of the Dead in Mexico* (University of Texas Press in cooperation with British Museum Press, 1991).

Child, Francis James, edited by Helen Child Sargent and George Lyman Kittredge. *English and Scottish Popular Ballads* (Boston: Houghton Mifflin, 1904).

Cohen, David, editor. *The Circle of Life: Rituals from the Human Family Album* (San Francisco: HarperSanFrancisco, 1991).

*Colman, Penny. *Corpses, Coffins, and Crypts: A History of Burial* (New York: Henry Holt and Company, 1997).

Cullen, Lisa Takeuchi. *Remember Me: A Lively Tour of the New American Way of Death* (New York: HarperCollins, 2006).

Editors of Time-Life Books. *Search for Immortality* (Alexandria, Va.: Time-Life Books, 1992).

Enright, D. J. *The Oxford Book of Death* (Oxford: Oxford University Press, 1983).

Garrison, Webb. *Strange Facts About Death* (Nashville: Abingdon, 1978).

Houdini, Harry. *A Magician Among the Spirits* (Amsterdam: Fredonia Books, 2002).

Hudson, Miles. *Assassination* (Sutton Publishing, 2000).

Huggett, Jane. *The Shaking of the Sheets: Death 1350–1660* (Bristol, England: Stuart Press, 1997).

Johnson, Marilyn. *The Deadbeat: Lost Souls, Lucky Stiffs, and the Perverse Pleasures of Obituaries* (New York: HarperCollins, 2006).

Kastenbaum, Robert and Beatrice. *Encyclopedia of Death: Myth, History, Philosophy,*

Science—The Many Aspects of Death and Dying (New York: Avon Books, 1993).

Lemley, Brad. "Shiny Happy People: Can You Reach Nirvana with the Aid of Science?" *Discover,* August 2006.

MacGregor, Geddes. *Images of Afterlife: Beliefs from Antiquity to Modern Times* (New York: Paragon House, 1992).

McNeill, Willian H., senior editor. *Berkshire Encyclopedia of World History,* volume 2. (Great Barrington, Mass.: Berkshire Publishing Group, 2005).

McQuade, Donald, et al., editors. *The Harper American Literature,* Volume 2, second edition (New York: HarperCollins, 1993).

Morgan, Ernest. *Dealing Creatively with Death: A Manual of Death Education and Simple Burial* (Hinesburg, Vt.: Upper Access, 2001).

*Prior, Natalie Jane. *The Encyclopedia of Preserved People: Pickled, Frozen, and Mummified Corpses from Around the World* (New York: Crown, 2002).

Roach, Mary. *Spook: Science Tackles the Afterlife* (New York: W. W. Norton, 2005).

———. *Stiff: The Curious Lives of Human Cadavers* (New York: W. W. Norton, 2003).

Rogak, Lisa. *Death Warmed Over: Funeral Food, Rituals, and Customs from Around the World* (Berkeley/Toronto: Ten Speed Press, 2004).

Rushton, Lucy. *Death Customs* (New York: Thomson Learning, 1993).

Schechter, Harold, and David Everitt. *The A to Z Encyclopedia of Serial Killers* (New York: Pocket Books, 1996).

Skal, David J. *Death Makes a Holiday: A Cultural History of Halloween* (New York: Bloomsbury, 2002).

Taylor, Richard P. *Death and the Afterlife: A Cultural Encyclopedia* (Santa Barbara: ABC-CLIO, 2000).

Taylor, Timothy. *The Buried Soul: How Humans Invented Death* (Boston: Beacon Press, 2002).

*Thornhill, Jan. *I Found a Dead Bird: The Kids' Guide to the Cycle of Life and Death* (Toronto: Maple Tree Press, 2006).

Turner, Alice K. *The History of Hell* (New York: Harcourt Brace, 1993).

*Walker, Richard. *The Right to Die?* (Mankato, Minn.: Sea-to-Sea Publications, 2006).

Weil, Elizabeth. "The Needle and the Damage Done," *New York Times Magazine,* February 11, 2007.

Weisberg, Barbara. *Talking to the Dead: Kate and Maggie Fox and the Rise of Spiritualism.* (New York: HarperCollins, 2004).

Welfare, Simon, and John Fairley. *Cabinet of Curiosities: A Delectable Assortment of Remarkable Tales and Outrageous Stories from All Over the World* (New York: St. Martin's Press, 1991).

Wicker, Christine. *Lily Dale: The True Story of the Town That Talks to the Dead* (San Francisco: HarperCollins, 2003).

*Wilcox, Charlotte. *Mummies, Bones, and Body Parts* (Minneapolis: Carolrhoda Books, 2000).

Wilentz, Sean, and Greil Marcus. *The Rose and the Briar: Death, Love and Liberty in the American Ballad* (New York: W. W. Norton, 2005).

Williams, Melvin G. *The Last Word: The Lure and Lore of Early New England Graveyards* (Boston: Oldstone Enterprises, 1973).

*Yeatts, Tabatha. *Forensics: Solving the Crime* (Minneapolis: Oliver Press, 2001).

*Asterisks indicate books for young readers.

http://news.nationalgeographic.com/news/index.html
www.nytimes.com
www.bbc.co.uk
www.cabinetmagazine.org
www.ringling.com
www.economist.com
www.assistedsuicide.org/suicide_laws.html
www.boston.com
www.who.int/en/
www.washingtonpost.com
www.time.com
www.westminster-abbey.org
www.china.org
www.spr.ac.uk
www.bpmlegal.com/wcoffin.html
www.exclassics.com/newgate/ngbibl.htm
www.cnn.com
www.ap.org
www.geomancy.net/resources/art/art-exhume.htm
http://content.nejm.org/cgi/content/full/357/4/328

ACKNOWLEDGMENTS

A great many people helped with this book, including Ellen Bourn, Lisa Goodfellow Bowe, John E. Chateauneuf, Laurel K. Gabel of the Association for Gravestone Studies, Jill Grinberg, Bree Detamore Harvey of Mount Auburn Cemetery, Draco LePage, Perseus LePage, Kelly Loughman, Michael Nelson, Ann-Marie Pucillo, Alison Kerr Miller, Blue Magruder of Harvard Museum of Natural History (and Thomas Scanlon for directing me to her), Ron Nagy of Lily Dale Museum, Kasha Ostbloom, Michaela Wayshak (who uncomplainingly endured more than her fair share of graveyard walks), Courtney Wayshak, Meg Winslow, and Kirsten Wolf.

And ever and especially—Kate O'Sullivan.

PICTURE CREDITS

Back jacket flap: Spike Mafford/Photodisc/Getty Images
Page(s)
v, viii, 11, 17, 27 (right), 29, 34, 57, 59, 60, 61, 63, 86, 116, 118 (bottom), 123, 133, 134: © Deborah Noyes
1: Museum of Anthropology, University of Missouri
2, 24 (both), 30, 42, 54, 70, 88, 110, 125, 128: © Deborah Noyes, courtesy Mount Auburn Cemetery
5, 98: The Print Collector/Heritage Images
15, 124: © Deborah Noyes, courtesy Harvard Museum of Natural History
16, 118 (top), 132: Library of Congress, Prints and Photographs Division
22: The Board of Trustees of the Armouries/Heritage Images
25, 81, 83: © Deborah Noyes, courtesy Lily Dale Assembly
27 (left): United States Patent Office
31: Courtesy of Alcor Life Extension Foundation
32: © Dmitrijs Mihejevs / Shutterstock
37: Peabody Museum of Archaeology and Ethnology
38: © skeletoriad / Shutterstock
40, 76: Erich Lessing/Art Resource, New York
48: The Bridgeman Art Library/Getty Images
52: Author's collection
74: Library of Congress/Prints and Photographs Division/McManus-Young Collection
85: Museum of London, Heritage Images
90: Smithsonian Art Museum/Washington, D.C./Art Resource, New York

INDEX

"Do not grieve, my friend — my dearest friend. I am ready to go, and — John, it will not be long." —Abigail Adams

"Bhikshus, never forget it: decay is inheren in all component things." —Buddh

"nothing but death." —jane Austen

"I can't sleep." —J. M. Barrie

"Soul, thou hast served Christ these *seventy years* and art thou *afraid to die?* Go out, soul, go out!" —Saint Hilary

"Why weep you? Did you think I should live forever? I thought dying had been harder." —King Louis XIV

"My God! My God! Why hast Thou forsaken me?... Father, into thy hands I commend my spirit . . . It is finished." —Jesus Christ

"So little done. So much to do!" —Alexander Graham Bell

"it is well." —george washington